BLOOM
Founded by | arihant

AF668790

Olympiad ACE

A Comprehensive Practice Book

for School Olympiads & Talent Search Exams

SOCIAL STUDIES

Class 9

by

Adhishree Neurgaonkar

Olympiad ACE

BLOOM
Bloom Cap Edu Ventures Pvt. Ltd.

Administrative & Production Office

'Ramchhaya' 4577/15, Agarwal Road, Darya Ganj, New Delhi -110002
Tele: 011- 47630600, 43518550

PRICE : ₹125.00

Published by Arihant Publications (I) Ltd.

For further information about the books log on to
www.bloomcap.org

Follow us on

Preface

"Future belongs to those Who prepares for it today"

School Olympiads are National & International level competitions conducted by different Government, Non-Government & Educational Organisations with the purpose of making the children ready to face competitive exams.

The challenging Questions asked in Olympiads motivate them to learn more & more and bring out the best results with improved academic performance. The Awards & Scholarship offered by Olympiads motivate children to aspire & strive for doing better and emerge out to be the best.

Social Studies Olympiads

Social Studies provides students with a comprehensive understanding of society, politics, economics and history. Studying Social Studies helps students understand the complexities of society, and prepares them for careers in fields such as public service, education, law, journalism, and research.

Social Studies Olympiads are meant to develop students' interest towards this vital subject.

'Bloom Social Studies Olympiad Study Book Class 9' is a perfect resource to Study & Practice for Olympiad Exams and other National & State Level Talent Search Exams & Other Competitions.

Some Special Features of Bloom Social Studies Olympiad Study Books are;

- Complete coverage of all the aspects of History, Geography and Civics.
- Chapterwise Exercises having different types of Objective Questions at par with the Olympiad Level.
- Olympiad Pattern Practice Sets at the end.

This book is prepared by Expert Panel with the utmost care, still if you have any suggestions regarding its improvement then feel free to contact us at support@bloomcap.org. We will try to inculcate your suggestions in the further editions.

Contents

Chapter 01

The French Revolution

MCQs 1 Mark Questions

1. The city of Paris was in the state of alarm on which date?
(a) 14th July, 1789 (b) 14th July, 1979
(c) 25th June, 1789 (d) 27th August, 1799

2. When did the Louis XVI became the King of France?
(a) 1772 (b) 1774
(c) 1775 (d) 1778

3. How many American Colonies got Independence by the help of Louis XVI?
(a) 10 (b) 12 (c) 13 (d) 15

4. The society and institution of France before 1789 is considered as ....
(a) monarchy (b) old regime
(c) feudal (d) democratic

5. What were the taxes called which were extracted by the Church from the peasants?
(a) Livre (b) Tithes
(c) Taille (d) All of these

6. The 18th century witnessed the emergence of which new social group in France?
(a) Middle class (b) Nobility
(c) Working class (d) None of these

7. Who authored 'Two Treaties of Government', which criticised the doctrine of divine and absolute right of the Monarch (King)?
(a) John Locke (b) Rousseau
(c) Montesquieu (d) Mirabeau

8. Which of the following refers to the political body representing the three Estates of pre-revolutionary France?
(a) Estates General
(b) Estates Committee
(c) National Assembly
(d) Parliament of France

9. The National Assembly framed a Constitution in 1791, to limit the power of the ....
(a) Third Estate (b) Monarch
(c) peasants (d) businessman

10. Who among the following wrote a book 'A Declaration of the Right of Women and Citizens'?
(a) Robespierre (b) Olympe de Gouges
(c) Jean-Paul Marat (d) Montesquieu

11. The National Anthem, Marseillaise was composed by ....
(a) Roget de L'Isle (b) Rousseau
(c) Mirabeau (d) Abbe Sieyes

12. Why was Louis XVI sentenced to death ?
(a) On the charge of treason.
(b) On the charge of discrimination.
(c) He was a cruel ruler.
(d) All of the above

13. At which place, Louis XVI was executed publically on 21st January, 1793?
(a) Paris (b) Place de la Concorde
(c) Versailles (d) Bastille

14. Why is the period from 1793-1794, referred to as the 'Reign of Terror'?
(a) Jacobins opted for loot and plunder.
(b) Louis XVI's successor became a tyrant.
(c) Robespierre followed a policy of severe control and punishment.
(d) None of the above

15. What was the reason(s) due to which the women of France were disappointed with the Constitution of 1791?
(a) They were forced to work a seamstresses.
(b) They did not have property right.
(c) They had no political rights.
(d) All of the above

16. Who among the following re-introduced slavery in France, after it was abolished by Jacobin regime?
(a) Napolean
(b) Louis XVI
(c) Olympe de Gouges
(d) Roget de L'Isle

17. Where did a triangular slave trade take place beside Europe and America?
(a) Africa (b) Australia
(c) Asia (d) All of these

18. What factor led to the rise of Napoleon?
(a) Fall of the Jacobin Government
(b) Robespierre's Reign of Terror
(c) Political instability of the directory
(d) Nationalist forces

19. Which among the following was/were introduced by Napoleon?
(a) Protection of private property
(b) Uniform system of weights and measures
(c) Both (a) and (b)
(d) None of the above

20. Napoleon was defeated in the Battle of .... in 1815.
(a) Austerlitz (b) Waterloo
(c) Sixth Coalition (d) Second Coalition

21. What does the given picture signify ?

(a) The Reign of Terror gives justice
(b) Parisian women on their way to Versailles
(c) Women queuing up at a bakery
(d) The emancipation of slaves

22. Consider the following statements and select the correct ones.
(a) Tax to be paid directly to the state in French society is known as Tithe.
(b) The book 'The Spirit of Law' was written by Montesquieu.
(c) The Representative of Third Estate were led by John Locke.
(d) All of the above

23. Identify the incorrectly matched pair.
(a) Louis XVI ascended the throne of France – 1804
(b) French Revolution took place – 1789
(c) Monarchy abolished in France – 1792
(d) Robespierre arrested and executed – 1794

24. Complete the given analogy.
Louis XVI : 1774 : : Napoleon : ?
(a) 1794 (b) 1804
(c) 1792 (d) 1815

25. What is the name of the couple given in the picture?

(a) Sans-culottes Couple
(b) Jacobin Couple
(c) Noble Couple
(d) Revolutionary Couple

MCQs 2 Marks Questions

26. Arrange the following events in chronological order.
I. Napoleon became Emperor
II. France became a Republic
III. Battle of Waterloo

Codes
(a) II, I, III (b) I, II, III
(c) III, I, II (d) II, III, I

27. Match the following.

	List I		List II
A.	Emancipation of slaves	1.	1794
B.	Slavery abolished in French Colonies	2.	1792
C.	France declared a republic	3.	1848
D.	Women won the Right to Vote in France	4.	1946

Codes

	A	B	C	D
(a)	1	3	2	4
(b)	4	3	2	1
(c)	1	2	3	4
(d)	3	1	4	2

28. Read the given statements associated with French Revolution and select which ones are true (T) and which ones are false (F).
I. On 5th May, 1789, Louis XVI called together an assembly of the Estates General to pass proposals for new taxes.
II. The National Assembly completed the draft of the Constitution in 1793.
III. The Constitution began with a declaration of the Rights of Man and Citizen.

Codes

	I	II	III		I	II	III
(a)	T	F	T	(b)	T	T	F
(c)	T	F	F	(d)	F	T	T

29. There are two statements marked as Assertion (A) and Reason (R). Mark your answer as per the codes given below.

Assertion (A) The Constitution of 1791, vested the power to make laws in the National Assembly, which was indirectly elected.

Reason (R) The members of the Jacobin Club belonged mainly to the less prosperous sections of society.

Codes
(a) Both A and R are true and R is the correct explanation of A
(b) Both A and R are true, but R is not the correct explanation of A
(c) A is true, but R is false
(d) A is false, but R is true

30. Identify the personality from the following information.

- In the book 'The Social Contract', he proposed the form of the government based on social contract between people and their representative.
- His writing played a significant role in bringing about French Revolution and encourage people to fight for their rights.

(a) John Locke (b) Rousseau
(c) Montesquieu (d) Mirabeau

31. Consider the following statements and select the correct option.

I. The French Revolution was started on the 5th May, 1789.
II. Women were active participants from the beginning, which brought important changes in the country of France.
III. Mirabeau was born in a noble family, but discorded his feudal privileges.

Codes

(a) Only I (b) II and III
(c) I and II (d) All of these

32. Arrange in chronological order.

I. Louis XVI becomes the King of France
II. French Revolution took place
III. National Assembly voted to declare war against Prussia and Austria

Codes

(a) I, II, III (b) II, III, I
(c) III, I, II (d) III, II, I

33. Read the following statements and select the correct option.

Statement (I) In the summer of 1792, the Jacobins planned an insurrection of a large number of Parisians, who were angered by the short supplies and high prices of food.

Statement (II) Robespierre pursued his policies so relentlessly that even his supporters began to demand moderation.

Codes

(a) Both statements I and II are correct
(b) Both statements I and II are incorrect
(c) Statement I is correct, but statement II is incorrect
(d) Statement I is incorrect, but statement II is correct

Darken your choice with HB Pencil

1. ⓐ ⓑ ⓒ ⓓ	7. ⓐ ⓑ ⓒ ⓓ	13. ⓐ ⓑ ⓒ ⓓ	19. ⓐ ⓑ ⓒ ⓓ	25. ⓐ ⓑ ⓒ ⓓ	31. ⓐ ⓑ ⓒ ⓓ
2. ⓐ ⓑ ⓒ ⓓ	8. ⓐ ⓑ ⓒ ⓓ	14. ⓐ ⓑ ⓒ ⓓ	20. ⓐ ⓑ ⓒ ⓓ	26. ⓐ ⓑ ⓒ ⓓ	32. ⓐ ⓑ ⓒ ⓓ
3. ⓐ ⓑ ⓒ ⓓ	9. ⓐ ⓑ ⓒ ⓓ	15. ⓐ ⓑ ⓒ ⓓ	21. ⓐ ⓑ ⓒ ⓓ	27. ⓐ ⓑ ⓒ ⓓ	33. ⓐ ⓑ ⓒ ⓓ
4. ⓐ ⓑ ⓒ ⓓ	10. ⓐ ⓑ ⓒ ⓓ	16. ⓐ ⓑ ⓒ ⓓ	22. ⓐ ⓑ ⓒ ⓓ	28. ⓐ ⓑ ⓒ ⓓ	
5. ⓐ ⓑ ⓒ ⓓ	11. ⓐ ⓑ ⓒ ⓓ	17. ⓐ ⓑ ⓒ ⓓ	23. ⓐ ⓑ ⓒ ⓓ	29. ⓐ ⓑ ⓒ ⓓ	
6. ⓐ ⓑ ⓒ ⓓ	12. ⓐ ⓑ ⓒ ⓓ	18. ⓐ ⓑ ⓒ ⓓ	24. ⓐ ⓑ ⓒ ⓓ	30. ⓐ ⓑ ⓒ ⓓ	

Chapter 02

Socialism in Europe and the Russian Revolution

MCQs 1 Mark Questions

1. Who wanted a nation which tolerated all religions?
   (a) Liberals (b) Radicals
   (c) Conservatives (d) All of these

2. What was/were the objective(s) of the Liberals?
   (a) They opposed the uncontrolled power of dynastic rulers.
   (b) They did not want to safeguard the rights of individuals against women.
   (c) They did not want a nation which tolerated all religion.
   (d) All of the above

3. ...... wanted a nation in which government was based on the majority of a country's population.
   (a) Liberals (b) Conservatives
   (c) Radicals (d) Capitalist

4. What do you meant by Suffragette Movement?
   (a) To give women the Right to Vote
   (b) To give women the Right to Property
   (c) To give women the Right to Equality
   (d) All of the above

5. Where did the Giuseppe Mazzini conspire to bring about a revolution?
   (a) Italy (b) Germany
   (c) France (d) Russia

6. Karl Marx wanted workers to overthrough ....
   (a) capitalism
   (b) rule of private property
   (c) radicals
   (d) socialist

7. By 1905, where was the socialist and trade unionists formed a labour party?
   (a) France (b) Britain
   (c) Germany (d) Russia

8. In which year, the Russian Social Democratic Workers Party was formed?
   (a) 1914 (b) 1898
   (c) 1900 (d) 1905

9. Which among the following best signifies the word 'Duma'?
   (a) Russian First Parliament
   (b) Socialist Party
   (c) Labour Party
   (d) None of the above

10. Name the typical Soviet hat wore by soldier in the given picture.

(a) Budeonovka (b) Fedora
(c) Tril by (d) Snapback

11. Which year was known as 'Bloody Sunday'?
(a) 1914 (b) 1917 (c) 1905 (d) 1900

12. Name the majority group of the Russian Social Democratic Workers Party led by Lenin.
(a) Bolsheviks (b) Mensheviks
(c) Jadidists (d) None of these

13. The Central powers during the First World War included countries like Germany, Turkey and ....
(a) France (b) Austria
(c) Britain (d) Russia

14. Why did the February Revolution 1917 in Petrograd take place ?
(a) Acute shortage of food.
(b) People wanted Lenin as their leader
(c) Duma was dissolved
(d) All of the above

15. Who wanted the Bolshevik Party to be renamed as Communist Party to indicate its radical aims?
(a) Karl Marx (b) Lenin
(c) Stalin (d) Tsar Nicholas II

16. USSR as a State was created from the Russian Empire in December, 1922 by..... .
(a) Mensheviks
(b) Bolsheviks
(c) Stalin
(d) Tsar Nicholas II

17 Complete the given analogy.
Russian Revolution : 1917 : : World War I : ?
(a) 1919 (b) 1918
(c) 1917 (d) 1914

18. Who were regarded as Kulaks in Russia?
(a) Well to do peasants
(b) Muslim reformers
(c) Lawyers
(d) Skilled labours

19. Identify the personality shown in the picture given below.

(a) Joseph Stalin
(b) V Lenin
(c) Karl Marx
(d) Tsar Nicholas II

20. Which of the following pair is correctly matched?
(a) Communist Party formed – 1920
(b) Lenin persuaded the Petrograd Soviet – 1918
(c) Lenin return to Russia – 1920
(d) Formation of Comintern – 1921

MCQs 2 Marks Questions

21. Read the given statements and select which ones are true (T) and which ones are false (F).

I. Non-Bolshevik socialists, liberals and supporters of autocracy condemned the Bolshevik uprising.

II. Mensheviks became the only party to participate in the elections to the all Russian Congress of Soviets.

III. In November 1919, the Bolsheviks conducted the elections to the Constituent Assembly, but they failed to gain majority support.

IV. During 1918 and 1919, the 'greens' (Socialist Revolutionaries) and 'whites' (pro-Tsarists) controlled most of the Russian Empire.

Codes

	I	II	III	IV		I	II	III	IV
(a)	T	F	T	F	(b)	T	F	F	T
(c)	F	T	T	F	(d)	F	F	T	F

22. Consider the following statements and select the correct ones.

I. In Russia, many factories were set up in late 1890's because of railway expansion.

II. Robert Owen believed in setting up of a cooperative community.

III. The armies in First World War fought from two direction i.e. Eastern and Western.

Codes

(a) I and II (b) II and III
(c) I, II and III (d) I and III

23. There are two statements marked as Assertion (A) and Reason (R). Mark your answer as per the codes given below.

Assertion (A) Workers in England and Germany began forming associations to fight for better living and working conditions.

Reason (R) At the beginning of the 20th century, the vast majority of Russia's people were agriculturists.

Codes

(a) Both A and R are true and R is the correct explanation of A
(b) Both A and R are true, but R is not the correct explanation of A
(c) A is true, but R is false
(d) A is false, but R is true

24. Match the following.

List I	List II
A. Karl Marx	1. Leader of Bolshevik Party
B. Lenin	2. Ruler of Russia
C. Stalin	3. Father of Communism
D. Tsar Nicholas II	4. Collectivisation Programme

Codes

	A	B	C	D		A	B	C	D
(a)	1	2	3	4	(b)	3	1	4	2
(c)	2	3	4	1	(d)	4	3	2	1

25. Consider the following statements and select the correct ones.

I. During the Civil War, the Bolsheviks kept industries and banks nationalised.

II. The Bolsheviks were totally opposed to private property.

III. In cities, Bolsheviks enforced the partition of large houses according to family requirements.

Codes

(a) Only I
(b) I and II
(c) II and III
(d) All of the above

26. Identify the personality from the information given below.

He believed that to free themselves from capitalist exploitation, workers had to construct a radically socialist society, where all property was socially controlled.

(a) Karl Marx
(b) Friedrich Engels
(c) Tsar Nicholas II
(d) Vladimir Lenin

27. Identify the incorrect statement about Socialism in Russia.

I. Socialists in the countryside formed the Socialist Revolutionary Party in 1900.
II. Social democrats disagreed with Socialists Revolutionaries about peasants.
III. The Social Democratic Party was divided into two wings, the Bolsheviks and the Mensheviks.

Codes

(a) Only I
(b) Only II
(c) Only III
(d) None of the above

28. Read the following statements and select the correct option.

Statement (I) By 1927-1928, the towns in Soviet Russia were facing an acute problem of grain supplies.

Statement (II) Stalin, who headed the party after the death of Lenin, introduced firm emergency measures.

Codes

(a) Both statements I and II are correct
(b) Both statements I and II are incorrect
(c) Statement I is correct, but statement II is incorrect
(d) Statement I is incorrect, but statement II is correct

29. On the given map of world, identify the country name marked as A, which belonged to Allied power in the First World War.

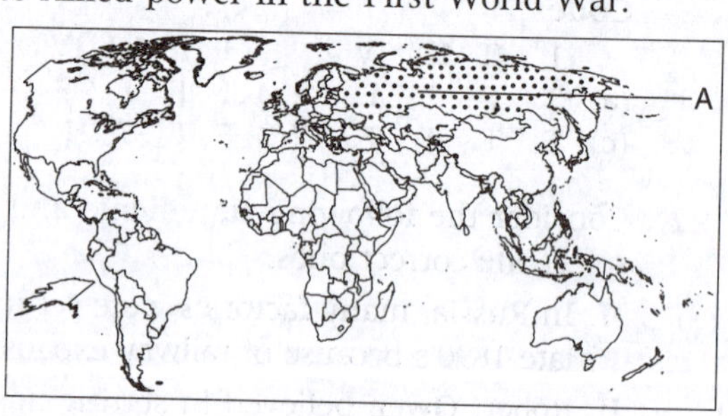

(a) England (b) Russia
(c) France (d) USA

Darken your choice with HB Pencil

1. ⓐ ⓑ ⓒ ⓓ	6. ⓐ ⓑ ⓒ ⓓ	11. ⓐ ⓑ ⓒ ⓓ	16. ⓐ ⓑ ⓒ ⓓ	21. ⓐ ⓑ ⓒ ⓓ	26. ⓐ ⓑ ⓒ ⓓ
2. ⓐ ⓑ ⓒ ⓓ	7. ⓐ ⓑ ⓒ ⓓ	12. ⓐ ⓑ ⓒ ⓓ	17. ⓐ ⓑ ⓒ ⓓ	22. ⓐ ⓑ ⓒ ⓓ	27. ⓐ ⓑ ⓒ ⓓ
3. ⓐ ⓑ ⓒ ⓓ	8. ⓐ ⓑ ⓒ ⓓ	13. ⓐ ⓑ ⓒ ⓓ	18. ⓐ ⓑ ⓒ ⓓ	23. ⓐ ⓑ ⓒ ⓓ	28. ⓐ ⓑ ⓒ ⓓ
4. ⓐ ⓑ ⓒ ⓓ	9. ⓐ ⓑ ⓒ ⓓ	14. ⓐ ⓑ ⓒ ⓓ	19. ⓐ ⓑ ⓒ ⓓ	24. ⓐ ⓑ ⓒ ⓓ	29. ⓐ ⓑ ⓒ ⓓ
5. ⓐ ⓑ ⓒ ⓓ	10. ⓐ ⓑ ⓒ ⓓ	15. ⓐ ⓑ ⓒ ⓓ	20. ⓐ ⓑ ⓒ ⓓ	25. ⓐ ⓑ ⓒ ⓓ	

Chapter 03

Nazism and the Rise of Hitler

MCQs 1 Mark Questions

1. After the World War II, an International Military Tribunal was set up to prosecute Nazi War criminals for ....
(a) crime against peace
(b) war crimes
(c) crimes against humanity
(d) All of the above

2. Which among the following fought against the Allied Powers?
(a) Germany
(b) Italy
(c) Japan
(d) All of the above

3. Which among the following started a Genocidal War before the World War II ?
(a) Russia
(b) Poland
(c) Austria
(d) Germany

4. What is the name of Republic that was established in Germany after World War I?
(a) German Republic State
(b) The Weimar Republic
(c) Republic of German Confederation
(d) German Federation

5. The Weimar Republic crushed the uprising with the help of a war veterans organisation called ....
(a) Bundestag
(b) Free Corps
(c) Duma
(d) Frankfurt

6. Identify the country that belonged to Allied Powers.
(a) Japan
(b) Italy
(c) America
(d) All of the above

7. What is not true about 'Peace of Treaty' of Versailles?
(a) Germany lost its overseas colonies.
(b) The Allied Powers demilitarised Germany to weaken its power.
(c) Germany was forced to pay compensation amounting to £ 12 million.
(d) None of the above

8. When Germany refused to pay compensation in 1923, ... occupied Germany's industrial area Ruhr (rich in coal).
(a) Russia (b) France
(c) England (d) Japan

9. Identify the country, which introduced the Dewas Plan that helped Germany to overcome the crisis.
(a) Russia
(b) Germany
(c) America
(d) England

10. After the Treaty of Versailles, Hitler joined which party in 1919?
(a) Nazi Party
(b) Worker's Party
(c) Bolshevik Party
(d) Socialist German Party

11. When did Hitler try to seize control of Bavaria and captured Berlin?
(a) 1919 (b) 1920
(c) 1923 (d) 1925

12. Which among the following was/were promise(s) made by Hitler?
(a) To give employment and a secure future for the youth.
(b) To remove foreign influences.
(c) To resist all foreign conspiracies against Germany.
(d) All of the above

13. What does the given picture signify?

(a) Desirable children that Hitler wanted to see.
(b) Jewish children arriving at a death factory to be gassed.
(c) Jewish students expelled from school.
(d) Unemployed youth in Germany.

14. Who among the following offered Chancellorship to Hitler in 1933?
(a) Hindenburg
(b) Churchill
(c) Helmuth
(d) Herbert Spencer

15. Complete the given analogy.
The Second World War started : 1939 : : Germany attacks USSR : ?
(a) 1944 (b) 1941
(c) 1946 (d) 1947

16. Identify what does the given picture suggest.

(a) Money is the God of Jews.
(b) To earn money, Jews committed the greatest crime.
(c) Jews do not rest, until they become the king of money.
(d) All of the above

17. Identify the correctly matched pair.
(a) Enabling Act was passed – 1933
(b) Hitler attack Soviet Union – 1943
(c) Tripartite Pact was signed – 1945
(d) Germany invaded Poland – 1930

18. Under fire decree, which of the following rights was/were suspended?
(a) Freedom of Speech
(b) Press
(c) Assembly
(d) All of the above

MCQs 2 Marks Questions

19. Read the following statements associated with establishment of racial state.

I. Nazis wanted only a society of pure and healthy Nordic German Aryans.

II. In Nazi Germany, Jews were the worst suffers.

Which of the above statements is/are correct?

(a) Only I
(b) Only II
(c) Both I and II
(d) Neither I nor II

20. Arrange the following events in chronological order.

I. Hitler became Chancellor of Germany
II. First World War ended
III. Hitler occupied Rhineland

Codes

(a) II, I, III
(b) III, I, II
(c) I, III, II
(d) III II I

21. Match the following.

List I	List II
A. 1938	1. Austria and Germany intergrated
B. January, 1945	2. Soviet troops liberate Auschwitz
C. 1918	3. Proclamation of the Weimar Republic
D. 1936	4. Nuremberg Rally wire held

Codes

	A	B	C	D
(a)	4	3	2	1
(b)	2	1	4	3
(c)	3	4	1	2
(d)	1	2	3	4

22. There are two statements marked as Assertion (A) and Reason (R). Mark your answer as per the codes given below.

Assertion (A) Special surveillance and security forces were created to control society in ways that the Nazis wanted.

Reason (R) On 30th January, 1933, President Hindenburg offered the Chancellorship, the highest position in the Cabinet of Ministers, to Hitler.

Codes

(a) Both A and R arc truc and R is the correct explanation of A
(b) Both A and R are true, but R is not the correct explanation of A
(c) A is true, but R is false
(d) A is false, but R is true

23. Identify the personality from the information given below.

- He promised to build a strong nation, undo the injustice of the Versailles Treaty.
- He acted as a messenger, corporal in the First World War.

(a) Stalin
(b) Hindenburg
(c) Hitler
(d) Churchill

24. Consider the following statements associated with Nazism and select which ones are true (T) and which ones are false (F).

I. The Youth League of the Nazis was founded in 1922.

II. The Nazi Regime used language and media with care and often to great effect.

III. Nazi ideas were spread through visual images, films, radio, posters, catchy slogans and leaflets.

Codes

	I	II	III
(a)	T	T	T
(b)	F	T	T
(c)	T	T	F
(d)	F	F	T

25. Arrange the following in chronological order.

I. The USSR and USA joined the Allied Powers

II. Germany surrendered to the Allies

III. Nuremberg Rally

Codes

(a) III, I, II

(b) III, II, I

(c) I, II, III

(d) II, III, I

26. Identify the correct statement(s).

I. Germany had fought the war largely on loans and had to pay war reparations in gold.

II. Puppet regimes which supported Hitler was established in a large part of Europe.

III. In Nazi Germany, women who maintained contacts with Jews, Polish or Russians were punished or imprisoned.

Codes

(a) Only I (b) I and II

(c) II and III (d) All of these

27. On the given world map, a country is marked as 'A' which was the part of Allied powers. Name the country.

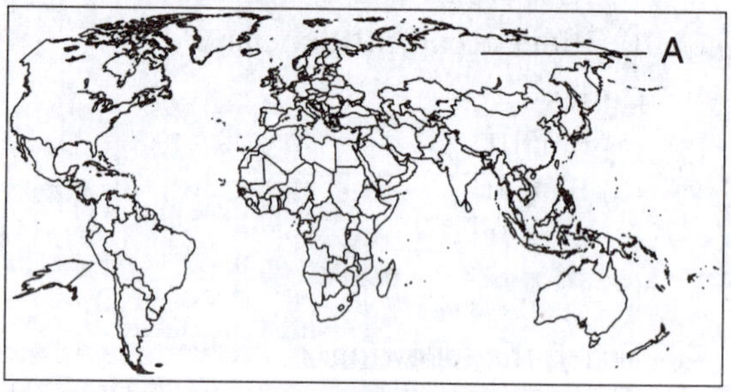

(a) France (b) Poland

(c) Germany (d) Former USSR

Darken your choice with HB Pencil

1. ⓐ ⓑ ⓒ ⓓ	6. ⓐ ⓑ ⓒ ⓓ	11. ⓐ ⓑ ⓒ ⓓ	16. ⓐ ⓑ ⓒ ⓓ	21. ⓐ ⓑ ⓒ ⓓ	26. ⓐ ⓑ ⓒ ⓓ
2. ⓐ ⓑ ⓒ ⓓ	7. ⓐ ⓑ ⓒ ⓓ	12. ⓐ ⓑ ⓒ ⓓ	17. ⓐ ⓑ ⓒ ⓓ	22. ⓐ ⓑ ⓒ ⓓ	27. ⓐ ⓑ ⓒ ⓓ
3. ⓐ ⓑ ⓒ ⓓ	8. ⓐ ⓑ ⓒ ⓓ	13. ⓐ ⓑ ⓒ ⓓ	18. ⓐ ⓑ ⓒ ⓓ	23. ⓐ ⓑ ⓒ ⓓ	
4. ⓐ ⓑ ⓒ ⓓ	9. ⓐ ⓑ ⓒ ⓓ	14. ⓐ ⓑ ⓒ ⓓ	19. ⓐ ⓑ ⓒ ⓓ	24. ⓐ ⓑ ⓒ ⓓ	
5. ⓐ ⓑ ⓒ ⓓ	10. ⓐ ⓑ ⓒ ⓓ	15. ⓐ ⓑ ⓒ ⓓ	20. ⓐ ⓑ ⓒ ⓓ	25. ⓐ ⓑ ⓒ ⓓ	

Chapter 04

Forest Society, Colonialism and Pastoralists in the Modern World

MCQs 1 Mark Questions

1. Why forests are important for human beings?
   (a) They enhance the quality of environment.
   (b) They provide natural resources for economic.
   (c) They also provide medicinal products.
   (d) All of the above

2. What do you understand by the term deforestation?
   (a) The disappearance of forests
   (b) Unplanned cutting of trees
   (c) Cutting trees for agriculture only
   (d) Cutting trees for industries

3. Where was the Imperial Forest Research Institute set up in 1906?
   (a) New Delhi (b) Bombay
   (c) Dehradun (d) Shimla

4. Which of the following trees was/were promoted for building ships or railways?
   (a) Teak and sal (b) Bushes and creepers
   (c) Fir and pines (d) Shisham

5. In Central America, shifting cultivation is also known as ....
   (a) Lading (b) Milpa
   (c) Chena (d) Chitemene

6. Why the colonial rulers considered forests as unproductive?
   (a) The forests were not fit for habitation.
   (b) Forest had wild grown trees only.
   (c) Forest did not yield revenue to enhance income of the state.
   (d) Forests were full of wild animals.

7. Bastar is located in which part of Chhattisgarh and borders Andhra Pradesh, Odisha and Maharashtra?
   (a) Northern
   (b) Southern
   (c) Western
   (d) Eastern

8. When did the Bastar Rebellion take place?
   (a) 1910 (b) 1912
   (c) 1922 (d) 1924

9. What do you understand by Nomad?
   (a) People who don't live at one place but move from one place to another to earn their living.
   (b) People who temporarily shift from one place to another.
   (c) People who live at one place and move from place to place to earn their living.
   (d) None of the above

10. In 19th century, where was Gujjar Bakarwals migrated and settled in search of pastures for their goat and sheep?

(a) Jammu and Kashmir
(b) Himachal Pradesh
(c) Uttarakhand
(d) Punjab

11. Identify the pastoralists given in the picture and name their settlement.

(a) Gujjar Mandap, Bakarwals
(b) Gaddi Mandap, Shepherd
(c) Sherpas, Kafila
(d) Bhotiyas, Mandap

12. Identify the option which signifies the word 'Bugyal'.

(a) A dry forest area
(b) Vast meadows in the high mountains
(c) High mountains in desert
(d) None of the above

13. Which among the following pastoral communities is found in Himachal Pradesh?

(a) Dhangars (b) Gaddi Shepherd
(c) Bhotiyas (d) Gollas

14. Which government converted pasture land into agricultural land to increase land revenue ?

(a) Central Government
(b) Colonial Government
(c) State Government
(d) Parliamentary Government

15. Complete the given analogy.
Kurumas : Karnataka : : Maldharis : ?

(a) Madhya Pradesh
(b) Rann of Kutch, Gujarat
(c) Odisha
(d) Rajasthan

16. During which season, the Dhangar Shepherd stayed in the Central plateau of Maharashtra?

(a) Winter (b) Summer
(c) Monsoon (d) Autumn

17. Rights that people got on the basis of tradition are known as ....

(a) Formal Rights
(b) Customary Rights
(c) Social Rights
(d) Personal Rights

18. Which among the following statements is/are correct about the Raika?

(a) The Raika (community) lived in the desert of Rajasthan.
(b) During the monsoons, the Raikas of Barmer, Jaisalmer, Jodhpur and Bikaner stayed in their home villages, where pasture was available.
(c) Maru Raikas herded camels and another group reared sheep and goat.
(d) All of the above

19. In the pre-colonial period, the Maasai society was divided into which of the following categories?

(a) Elders and warriors
(b) Maginoo and alipin
(c) Male and female
(d) Alipin and Maharlika

20. When did the Colonial Government in India passed the Criminal Tribes Act?

(a) 1850 (b) 1871
(c) 1875 (d) 1890

21. Complete the given analogy.
Birsa Munda : Chota Nagpur : : Sitarama Raju : ?
(a) Andhra Pradesh
(b) Maharashtra
(c) Odisha
(d) Chhattisgarh

22. Name the system of plantation shown in the picture

(a) Deodar plantation in kangra
(b) Shifting cultivation, Java
(c) Shifting cultivation, India
(d) Taungya cultivation, Thailand

23. Who among the following were an important pastoral community of Madhya Pradesh?
(a) Banjaras
(b) Dhangars
(c) Kalangs
(d) Pastoralists

24. What was/were the problem(s) the Maasai have to be faced?
(a) Loss of access to water sources for their herds.
(b) Continuous loss of their grazing lands.
(c) Lack of recognition of traditional territory and communal land holdings.
(d) All of the above

MCQs 2 Marks Questions

25. Arrange the following events in chronological order.
I. Enactment of Indian Forest Act
II. First Terrible Famine
III. Imperial Forest Research Institute was set up

Codes
(a) III, II, I
(b) II, I, III
(c) I, II, III
(d) II, III, I

26. Identify the correct statement(s) associated with land for cultivation.
I. In the process of commercialisation of agriculture during colonial period, peasants were forced to expand cultivation area.
II. Jute, sugar, wheat and cotton are the example of commercial crops.

Codes
(a) Only I
(b) Only II
(c) Both I and II
(d) Neither I nor II

27. Which of the following statements is/are correct?
I. The Kalangs of Java Island of Indonesia were a community of skilled forest cutters and shifting cultivators.
II. One of the major impacts of European colonialism was on the practice of shifting cultivation.

Codes
(a) Only I (b) Only II
(c) Both I and II (d) Neither I nor II

28. Arrange the following events in chronological order.

I. Report of Royal commission on agriculture
II. Tanganyika comes under British rule
III. Severe drought in Maasailand

Codes

(a) II, I, III (b) III, I, II
(c) I, III, II (d) II, I, III

29. Match the following.

List I	List II
A. The Mataram Kingdom of Java split into two kingdoms	1. 1755
B. Enactment of Indian Forest Act	2. 1865
C. Forest divided into three categories	3. 1878
D. Indian Forest Service was set up by Dietrich Brandis.	4. 1864

Codes

	A	B	C	D
(a)	4	3	2	1
(b)	3	2	4	1
(c)	1	2	3	4
d)	2	4	1	3

30. There are two statements marked as Assertion (A) and Reason (R). Mark your answer as per the codes given below.

Assertion (A) Java is now famous as a rice producing island in Indonesia.

Reason (R) When the Dutch began to gain control over the forests in 18th century. Java tried to make the Kalangas work under them.

Codes

(a) Both A and R are true and R is the correct explanation of A
(b) Both A and R are true, but R is not the correct explanation of A
(c) A is true, but R is false
(d) A is false, but R is true

31. There are two statements marked as Assertion (A) and Reason (R). Mark your answer as per the codes given below.

Assertion (A) The Banjaras are a nomadic group which live in the villages of Rajasthan, Punjab, Uttar Pradesh, Madhya Pradesh and Maharashtra.

Reason (R) The Banjaras move with their cattle over long distances in search of pasture lands.

Codes

(a) Both A and R are true and R is the correct explanation of A
(b) Both A and R are true, but R is not the correct explanation of A
(c) A is true, but R is false
(d) A is false, but R is true

32. Read the following statements associated with Gujjar Bakarwals of Jammu and Kashmir and select which ones are true (T) and which ones are false (F).

I. They move annually between their summer and winter grazing grounds in groups known as Kafila.
II. The Gujjar Bakarwals are herders of goat and sheep.
III. During the winters, when the Himalayas are covered with snow, they live in the foothills of the Siwalik Ranges.

Codes

	I	II	III
(a)	T	T	T
(b)	F	T	T
(c)	T	T	F
(d)	F	F	T

33. Which among the following statements is/are correct?

I. Maasai pastoralists mostly inhabit the parts of Tanzania and Kenya.

II. Railways were essential for colonial trade and for the movement of Imperial Troops.

III. To run locomotives, wood was needed as fuel and to lay railway lines sleepers were essential to hold the tracks together.

Codes

(a) Only I
(b) I and II
(c) II and III
(d) All of the above

34. Identify the tribe community of India with the help of information given below.

- They spent their winter in the low hills of Siwalik Range, grazing their flocks in scrub forests. By April, they moved North and spent the summer in Lahul and Spiti.
- When the snow melted and the high passes were clear, many of them moved on to higher mountain meadows.

(a) Dhangars
(b) Gaddi Shepherd
(c) The Gollas
(d) Gujjar Bakarwals

35. Identify the pair(s) which is/are correctly matched.

Local Name (Shifting Cultivation)		Country
I. Lading (Ladang)	–	South-East Asia
II. Penda	–	India
III. Chitemene or Tavy	–	Africa
IV. Chena	–	Sri Lanka

Codes

(a) Only I
(b) Both I and II
(c) I, II and III
(d) All of the above

Darken your choice with HB Pencil

1.	ⓐ ⓑ ⓒ ⓓ	7.	ⓐ ⓑ ⓒ ⓓ	13.	ⓐ ⓑ ⓒ ⓓ	19.	ⓐ ⓑ ⓒ ⓓ	25.	ⓐ ⓑ ⓒ ⓓ	31.	ⓐ ⓑ ⓒ ⓓ
2.	ⓐ ⓑ ⓒ ⓓ	8.	ⓐ ⓑ ⓒ ⓓ	14.	ⓐ ⓑ ⓒ ⓓ	20.	ⓐ ⓑ ⓒ ⓓ	26.	ⓐ ⓑ ⓒ ⓓ	32.	ⓐ ⓑ ⓒ ⓓ
3.	ⓐ ⓑ ⓒ ⓓ	9.	ⓐ ⓑ ⓒ ⓓ	15.	ⓐ ⓑ ⓒ ⓓ	21.	ⓐ ⓑ ⓒ ⓓ	27.	ⓐ ⓑ ⓒ ⓓ	33.	ⓐ ⓑ ⓒ ⓓ
4.	ⓐ ⓑ ⓒ ⓓ	10.	ⓐ ⓑ ⓒ ⓓ	16.	ⓐ ⓑ ⓒ ⓓ	22.	ⓐ ⓑ ⓒ ⓓ	28.	ⓐ ⓑ ⓒ ⓓ	34.	ⓐ ⓑ ⓒ ⓓ
5.	ⓐ ⓑ ⓒ ⓓ	11.	ⓐ ⓑ ⓒ ⓓ	17.	ⓐ ⓑ ⓒ ⓓ	23.	ⓐ ⓑ ⓒ ⓓ	29.	ⓐ ⓑ ⓒ ⓓ	35.	ⓐ ⓑ ⓒ ⓓ
6.	ⓐ ⓑ ⓒ ⓓ	12.	ⓐ ⓑ ⓒ ⓓ	18.	ⓐ ⓑ ⓒ ⓓ	24.	ⓐ ⓑ ⓒ ⓓ	30.	ⓐ ⓑ ⓒ ⓓ		

Chapter 05

Size, Location and Physical Features of India

MCQs 1 Mark Questions

1. The Northernmost longitude of India is
(a) 97°25′ N (b) 8°4′ E
(c) 82°32′ N (d) 37°6′ N

2. Which of the following parallel of latitudes divides India into two almost equal part?
(a) Equator (b) Tropic of Capricorn
(c) Tropic of Cancer (d) Prime Meridian

3. India's total area accounts for .... of the geographical area of the world.
(a) 2.9% (b) 3.2% (c) 2.4% (d) 4.2%

4. When did the Southernmost point of Indian Union 'Indira Point' got submerged under the sea water during Tsunami?
(a) 2002 (b) 2003
(c) 2004 (d) 2005

5. What is the length of Indian coastline?
(a) 8716 km (b) 7165 km
(c) 9515 km (d) 7516 km

6. Identify the geographical features which bounds India's mainland South of 22°N latitude.
(a) Young Fold Mountains
(b) Sandy Desert
(c) Lava Plateau
(d) Seas and ocean

7. Which meridian is fixed as Standard Meridian of India?
(a) $82\frac{1}{2}$° E (b) $84\frac{1}{2}$° E
(c) 86° E (d) $87\frac{1}{2}$° E

8. The Standard Meridian of India passes through which among the following places?
(a) Kanyakumari (Tamil Nadu)
(b) Walong (Arunachal Pradesh)
(c) Kutch (Gujarat)
(d) Mirzapur (Uttar Pradesh)

9. At which among the following places, there is least difference in duration between day and night time?
(a) Leh (b) Kanyakumari
(c) Itanagar (d) Srinagar

10. Identify the smallest neighbouring country of India.
(a) Nepal (b) Bhutan
(c) Sri Lanka (d) Bangladesh

11. .... are the water bodies which separate Sri Lanka from India.
(a) Palk strait and Gulf of Khambat
(b) Palk strait and Gulf of Mannar
(c) Strait of Gibralter
(d) Sunda Strait

12. Identify the incorrectly matched pair.
(a) West Bengal – Border with Bangladesh
(b) Gujarat – Border with Pakistan
(c) Bihar – Border with China
(d) Uttarakhand – Border with Nepal

13. What is landmass bounded by sea on three sides called?
(a) Coast (b) Island
(c) Peninsula (d) None of these

14. The Himalayan mountains form an arc and cover distance of ....
(a) 2400 km (b) 1500 km
(c) 2700 km (d) 6000 km

15. Which of the following valleys marks the Eastern most boundary of the Himalayas?
(a) Chenab Valley
(b) Brahmaputra Valley
(c) Parvati Valley
(d) Kangra and Kulu Valley

16. Identify the average height of Himadri (Great Himalayas), the most continuous range of Himalaya.
(a) 4000 km (b) 5000 km
(c) 6000 km (d) 8000 km

17. The folds of the great Himalayas are .... in nature.
(a) symmetrical
(b) asymmetrical
(c) spherical
(d) Both (a) and (b)

18. What is/are the major river system behind the formation of the Northern plain?
(a) Indus (b) Ganga
(c) Brahmaputra (d) All of these

19. How much area is covered by the Northern plain?
(a) 3 lakh sq km (b) 5 lakh sq km
(c) 7 lakh sq km (d) 9 lakh sq km

20. What is the region between Kali and Teesta rivers called?
(a) Kumaon Himalayas
(b) Nepal Himalayas
(c) Assam Himalayas
(d) Himachal Himalayas

21. Majuli is the largest inhabited riverine islands in the world. It lies in which of the following rivers?
(a) Indus (b) Brahmaputra
(c) Ganga (d) Ghaggar

22. What was formed due to the breaking up and drifting of Gondwana land?
(a) Peninsular Plateau
(b) Deccan Plateau
(c) Coastal Plains
(d) Central Highlands

23. Which of the following is the highest peak of Western Ghats?
(a) Anai Mudi (b) Mahendragiri
(c) Dhaulagiri (d) Kamet

24. What is/are the feature(s) of Western Ghats?
(a) Western Ghats lie parallel to the Western coast.
(b) They are continuous and can be crossed through passes only.
(c) The Western Ghats are higher than the Eastern Ghats.
(d) All of the above

25. The Indian desert lies towards the Western margins of the ....
(a) Shiwalik Hills (b) Jaintia Hills
(c) Aravali Hills (d) Khasi Hills

26. Name the only river that is found in desert region of India.
(a) Tapti (b) Krishna
(c) Luni (d) Narmada

27. Complete the given analogy.
Tributary of Indus : Jhelum :: Tributary of the Ganga : ?
(a) Subansiri (b) Ghaggar
(c) Beas (d) Ravi

28. Which of the following is the innermost range of Himalayas?
(a) Himadri (b) Shiwalik
(c) Pir Panjal (d) Purvancha

29. India is bounded by which of the following mountains in the North-West, North and North-East?
(a) Dome Mountains
(b) Young Fold Mountains
(c) Black Mountains
(d) Volcanic Mountainsl

MCQs 2 Marks Questions

30. Consider the following statements and choose the correct option.
I. The landmass of India has an area of 3.28 million sq km.
II. India's total area accounts for about 2.4 per cent of the total geographical area of the world.
III. India is the 7th largest country of the world.
Codes
(a) Only I (b) I and II
(c) II and III (d) All of these

31. Match the following.

List I (Peaks)	List II (Height in metre)
A. Makalu	1. 8078 m
B. Annapurna	2. 8481 m
C. Kanchenjunga	3. 8598 m
D. Nanda Devi	4. 7817 m

Codes

	A	B	C	D
(a)	2	1	3	4
(b)	3	2	1	4
(c)	1	2	3	4
(d)	1	4	3	2

32. Arrange the following mountain peaks in ascending order.
I. Dhaulagiri
II. Nanga Parbat
III. Nanda Devi
Codes
(a) I, II, III (b) III, II, I
(c) I, III, II (d) II, I, III

33. There are two statements marked as Assertion (A) and Reason (R). Mark your answer as per the codes given below.
Assertion (A) The Ganga plain extends between Ghaggar and Teesta rivers.
Reason (R) The Ganga plain spreads over North India in Haryana, Delhi, Uttar Pradesh, Bihar, partly Jharkhand and West Bengal.
Codes
(a) Both A and R are true and R is the correct explanation of A
(b) Both A and R are true, but R is not the correct explanation of A
(c) A is true, but R is false
(d) A is false, but R is true

34. Consider the following statements associated with Coastal Plains and select which ones are true (T) and which ones are false (F).
I. The Peninsular Plateau is flanked by stretch of narrow coastal strips.
II. The Western Coast sandwiched between the Western Ghats and the Arabian Sea is a narrow plain.
III. The Northern part of the coast is called the Konkan (Mumbai-Goa) and the Central Stretch is called the Kannad Plain.
IV. The plains along the Bay of Bengal are wide and level (gentle).
Codes

	I	II	III	IV
(a)	T	T	T	T
(b)	F	T	T	F
(c)	T	T	F	F
(d)	F	F	T	T

35. Consider the following statements and choose the correct option.

I. The rivers coming from Northern mountains are involved in depositional work.

II. The Western part of the Northern plains is referred to as the Punjab plains.

III. The largest part of the Northern plains is formed of older alluvium.

Codes

(a) Only I
(b) I and II
(c) II and III
(d) All of the above

36. Identify the geographical feature from the information given below.

- It is a tableland composed of the old crystalline, igneous and metamorphic rocks.
- It was formed due to the breaking and drifting of the Gondwana land and thus, making it a part of the oldest landmass.

(a) The Peninsula Plateaus
(b) The Coastal Plains
(c) The Northern Plains
(d) The Islands

37. On the given map of India, identify the mountain which is marked as A.

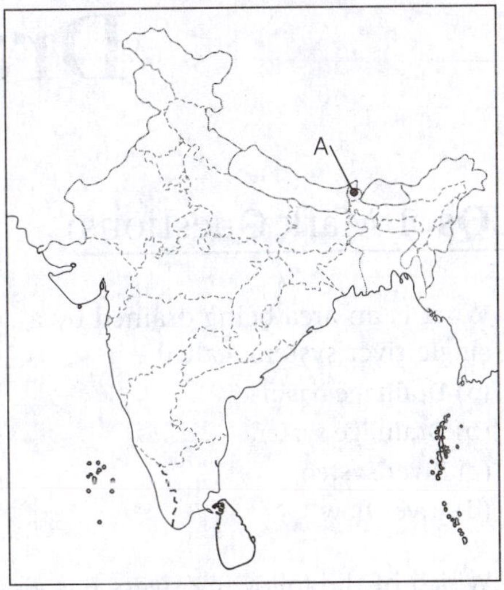

(a) Anai Mudi (b) Kanchenjunga
(c) Mount Everest (d) Dhaulagiri

Darken your choice with HB Pencil

1.	ⓐ ⓑ ⓒ ⓓ	8.	ⓐ ⓑ ⓒ ⓓ	15.	ⓐ ⓑ ⓒ ⓓ	22.	ⓐ ⓑ ⓒ ⓓ	29.	ⓐ ⓑ ⓒ ⓓ	36.	ⓐ ⓑ ⓒ ⓓ
2.	ⓐ ⓑ ⓒ ⓓ	9.	ⓐ ⓑ ⓒ ⓓ	16.	ⓐ ⓑ ⓒ ⓓ	23.	ⓐ ⓑ ⓒ ⓓ	30.	ⓐ ⓑ ⓒ ⓓ	37.	ⓐ ⓑ ⓒ ⓓ
3.	ⓐ ⓑ ⓒ ⓓ	10.	ⓐ ⓑ ⓒ ⓓ	17.	ⓐ ⓑ ⓒ ⓓ	24.	ⓐ ⓑ ⓒ ⓓ	31.	ⓐ ⓑ ⓒ ⓓ		
4.	ⓐ ⓑ ⓒ ⓓ	11.	ⓐ ⓑ ⓒ ⓓ	18.	ⓐ ⓑ ⓒ ⓓ	25.	ⓐ ⓑ ⓒ ⓓ	32.	ⓐ ⓑ ⓒ ⓓ		
5.	ⓐ ⓑ ⓒ ⓓ	12.	ⓐ ⓑ ⓒ ⓓ	19.	ⓐ ⓑ ⓒ ⓓ	26.	ⓐ ⓑ ⓒ ⓓ	33.	ⓐ ⓑ ⓒ ⓓ		
6.	ⓐ ⓑ ⓒ ⓓ	13.	ⓐ ⓑ ⓒ ⓓ	20.	ⓐ ⓑ ⓒ ⓓ	27.	ⓐ ⓑ ⓒ ⓓ	34.	ⓐ ⓑ ⓒ ⓓ		
7.	ⓐ ⓑ ⓒ ⓓ	14.	ⓐ ⓑ ⓒ ⓓ	21.	ⓐ ⓑ ⓒ ⓓ	28.	ⓐ ⓑ ⓒ ⓓ	35.	ⓐ ⓑ ⓒ ⓓ		

Chapter 06

Drainage

MCQs 1 Mark Questions

1. What is an area being drained by a single river system, called ?
   (a) Drainage basin
   (b) Drainage system
   (c) River system
   (d) River flow

2. Which of the following rivers has world's largest drainage basin?
   (a) Amazon (b) The Ganga
   (c) Nile (d) Narmada

3. Indian rivers can be divided into how many groups?
   (a) Two (b) Three
   (c) Four (d) Five

4. Which among the following is a perennial river?
   (a) Brahmaputra (b) Narmada
   (c) Godavari (d) Tapi

5. The Indus River flows Southwards till it reaches the Arabian Sea near which city of Pakistan?
   (a) Sindh
   (b) Islamabad
   (c) Karachi
   (d) Lahore

6. The river Bhagirathi is known as Ganga, when it joined river Alaknanda at ....
   (a) Karnaprayag
   (b) Rudraprayag
   (c) Devprayag
   (d) None of the above

7. Identify a tributary of Brahmaputra from the given options.
   (a) Kosi (b) Lohit
   (c) Koyana (d) Musi

8. Where was the most Peninsular rivers originate and flow towards the Bay of Bengal?
   (a) Eastern Ghats
   (b) Western Ghats
   (c) Himalaya
   (d) Tibet

9. Name the river which originates in the Amarkantak Hills (Madhya Pradesh).
   (a) Tapi
   (b) Narmada
   (c) Godavari
   (d) Kaveri

10. Name the river which is also known as Dakshin Ganga.
    (a) Mahanadi (b) Krishna
    (c) Kaveri (d) Godavari

11. Identify the tributary/tributaries of Godavari river.
(a) Purna (b) Wardha
(c) Pranhita (d) All of these

12. Mahanadi river originate in the highlands of ....
(a) Odisha
(b) Jharkhand
(c) Chhattisgarh
(d) Madhya Pradesh

13. Which among the following is the tributary of the River Krishna?
(a) Tungabhadra (b) Amravati
(c) Bhavani (d) Kabini

14. Which river originated from the Western Ghats near Mahabaleshwar?
(a) Mahanadi (b) Krishna
(c) Kaveri (d) Narmada

15. What is the total length of the Krishna river ?
(a) 1400 km (b) 1500 km
(c) 760 km (d) 2025 km

16. Which river makes the second biggest waterfall in India, known as 'Shivasamudram'?
(a) Krishna (b) Kaveri
(c) Godavari (d) Narmada

17. Which one of the following options best signifies this image?

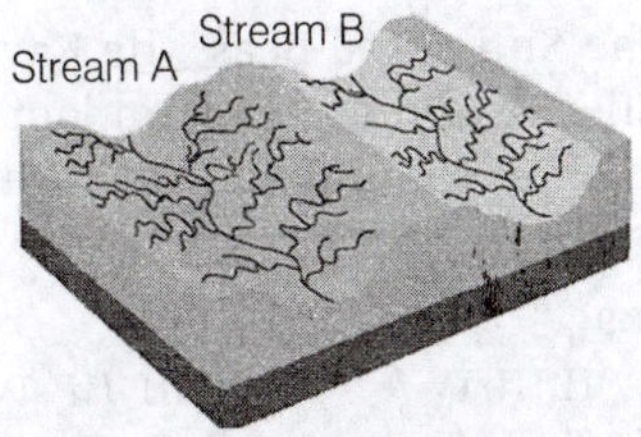

(a) River Basin (b) Drainage Basin
(c) Water Divide (d) River System

18. Sambhar Salt lake is located in which state?
(a) Odisha (b) Rajasthan
(c) Chhattisgarh (d) Madhya Pradesh

19. Identify the lake(s) which is/are located in Odisha.
(a) Wular lake (b) Chilika lake
(c) Sambhar lake (d) All of these

20. .... is fresh water lake, located in Jammu and Kashmir.
(a) Kolleru lake (b) Pulicat lake
(c) Wular lake (d) Chilika lake

21. Which of the following statements is not correct about origination of the rivers?
(a) The river Indus rises in Tibet near lake Mansarovar.
(b) The Godavari is the largest Peninsular river.
(c) The Narmada rises in the Amarkantak Hills in Kerala.
(d) None of the above

22. Complete the given analogy.
Kolleru Lake : Andhra Pradesh : : Vembanad Lake : ?
(a) Tamil Nadu (b) Kerala
(c) Karnataka (d) Telangana

MCQs 2 Marks Questions

23. Which of the following statements is/are correct?
I. The term drainage describes the river system of an area.
II. The drainage systems of India are mainly controlled by the broad relief features of the sub-continent.

Codes
(a) Only I (b) Only II
(c) Both I and II (d) Neither I nor II

24. Arrange the following rivers in sequence as per their length.

I. Ganga
II. Kaveri
III. Godavari

Codes

(a) I, II, III (b) III, II, I
(c) I, III, II (d) II, I, III

25. Match the following.

List I (Rivers)	List II (Tributaries)
A. Indus	1. Yamuna
B. Ganga	2. Sutlej
C. Krishna	3. Manjra
D. Godavari	4. Bhima

Codes

	A	B	C	D		A	B	C	D
(a)	2	1	4	3	(b)	4	3	2	1
(c)	4	3	1	2	(d)	3	4	2	1

26. There are two statements marked as Assertion (A) and Reason (R). Mark your answer as per the codes given below.

Assertion (A) Most of the freshwater lakes are in the Himalayan region.

Reason (R) Freshwater lake are of glacial origin. They formed when glaciers dug out a basin, which was later filled with snowmelt.

Codes

(a) Both A and R are true and R is the correct explanation of A
(b) Both A and R are true, but R is not the correct explanation of A
(c) A is true, but R is false
(d) A is false, but R is true

27. Consider the following statements and choose the correct option.

I. The Mahanadi rises in the Brahmagiri range of the Western Ghats.
II. Water from rivers is a basic natural resource, essential for various human activities.
III. The Tapi rises in the Satpura ranges, in the Betul district of Madhya Pradesh.

Codes

(a) Only I (b) I and II
(c) II and III (d) All of these

28. Match the following.

List I (Rivers)	List II (Lengths)
A. Mahanadi	1. 860 km
B. Ganga	2. 2500 km
C. Indus	3. 2900 km
D. Kaveri	4. 760 km

Codes

	A	B	C	D		A	B	C	D
(a)	2	1	4	3	(b)	4	3	2	1
(c)	1	2	3	4	(d)	3	4	2	1

29. Consider the following statements associated with the Himalayan rivers and select which ones are true (T) and which ones are false (F).

I. The major Himalayan rivers are the Indus, the Ganga and the Brahmaputra.
II. Himalayan rivers are long and are joined by many large and important tributaries.
III. The Indus flows through Baltistan and Gilgit and emerges from the mountains at Attock.
IV. The Sutlej, the Beas, the Ravi, the Chenab and the Jhelum join together to enter the Indus near Mithankot in Pakistan.

Codes

	I	II	III	IV		I	II	III	IV
(a)	T	T	T	T	(b)	F	T	T	F
(c)	T	T	F	F	(d)	F	F	T	T

30. Identify the river basin from the information given below.

- It rises from the slopes of the Western Ghats in the Nasik district of Maharashtra. Its length is about 1500 km.
- It drains into the Bay of Bengal. Its drainage basin is also the largest among the Peninsular rivers.

(a) The Godavari Basin
(b) The Narmada Basin
(c) The Krishna Basin
(d) The Kaveri Basin

31. Choose the incorrect statement(s).

I. The Krishna flows for about 1400 km and reaches the Bay of Bengal.
II. A meandering river across a flood plain form set-offs that later develops into ox-bow lakes.
III. The main tributaries of the Krishna Basin are Amravati, Bhavani, Hemavati and Kabini.

Codes

(a) Only I (b) I and II
(c) Only III (d) All of these

32. Identify the lake which is marked as 'A' on the given map of India.

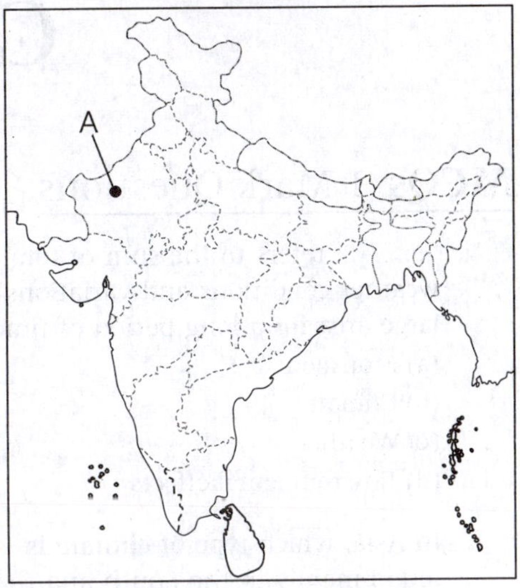

(a) Pulicat Lake (b) Sambhar Lake
(c) Wular Lake (d) Dal Lake

Darken your choice with HB Pencil

1.	ⓐ ⓑ ⓒ ⓓ	7.	ⓐ ⓑ ⓒ ⓓ	13.	ⓐ ⓑ ⓒ ⓓ	19.	ⓐ ⓑ ⓒ ⓓ	25.	ⓐ ⓑ ⓒ ⓓ	31.	ⓐ ⓑ ⓒ ⓓ
2.	ⓐ ⓑ ⓒ ⓓ	8.	ⓐ ⓑ ⓒ ⓓ	14.	ⓐ ⓑ ⓒ ⓓ	20.	ⓐ ⓑ ⓒ ⓓ	26.	ⓐ ⓑ ⓒ ⓓ	32.	ⓐ ⓑ ⓒ ⓓ
3.	ⓐ ⓑ ⓒ ⓓ	9.	ⓐ ⓑ ⓒ ⓓ	15.	ⓐ ⓑ ⓒ ⓓ	21.	ⓐ ⓑ ⓒ ⓓ	27.	ⓐ ⓑ ⓒ ⓓ		
4.	ⓐ ⓑ ⓒ ⓓ	10.	ⓐ ⓑ ⓒ ⓓ	16.	ⓐ ⓑ ⓒ ⓓ	22.	ⓐ ⓑ ⓒ ⓓ	28.	ⓐ ⓑ ⓒ ⓓ		
5.	ⓐ ⓑ ⓒ ⓓ	11.	ⓐ ⓑ ⓒ ⓓ	17.	ⓐ ⓑ ⓒ ⓓ	23.	ⓐ ⓑ ⓒ ⓓ	29.	ⓐ ⓑ ⓒ ⓓ		
6.	ⓐ ⓑ ⓒ ⓓ	12.	ⓐ ⓑ ⓒ ⓓ	18.	ⓐ ⓑ ⓒ ⓓ	24.	ⓐ ⓑ ⓒ ⓓ	30.	ⓐ ⓑ ⓒ ⓓ		

Chapter 07

Climate

MCQs 1 Mark Questions

1. .... refers to the sum of total weather conditions and variations over a large area for a long period of time.
   (a) Monsoon
   (b) Climate
   (c) Weather
   (d) Environmental effects

2. In Asia, which type of climate is found mainly in the South and the South-East?
   (a) Tundra (b) Monsoon
   (c) Oceanic (d) All of these

3. What is the annual precipitation in Ladakh?
   (a) 400 cm (b) Less than 10 cm
   (c) 200 cm (d) 100 cm

4. Choose the incorrect statement from the given options.
   (a) Coastal areas experience less contrasts in temperature.
   (b) Seasonal contrasts are more in the interior of the country.
   (c) Most parts of the country receive rainfall from April to June.
   (d) The variations in seasons have given rise to variety in lives of people.

5. Which one of the following is not one of the six major controls of the climate of any place?
   (a) Latitude
   (b) Temperature
   (c) Pressure and wind system
   (d) Distance from the sea

6. In which of the following months does the Tamil Nadu Coast get most of its rainfall?
   (a) December and February
   (b) October and November
   (c) March and May
   (d) June and September

7. Due to the curvature of the Earth, the amount of solar energy received varies according to ....
   (a) latitude
   (b) altitudes
   (c) pressure and winds
   (d) All of the above

8. Who were the traders that came to India and named the seasonal reversal of wind system as 'Monsoon'?
   (a) Arabs
   (b) French
   (c) Portuguese
   (d) British

9. Name the line passes from the Rann of Kuchchh in the West to Mizoram in the East.
   (a) Equator
   (b) Tropic of Capricorn
   (c) Tropic of Cancer
   (d) Arctic circle

10. Which among the following is responsible for deflecting winds towards right in the Northern Hemisphere and towards left in the Southern Hemisphere?
(a) Relief
(b) Monsoon
(c) Centripetal force
(d) Coriolis force

11. Identify the winds which blow over the warm oceans, gather moisture and bring widespread rainfall over the mainland of India.
(a) Monsoon winds
(b) South-East monsoon winds
(c) South-West monsoon winds
(d) Kal Baishakhi

12. Which type of climate is characterised by a distinct seasonal pattern?
(a) Monsoon type
(b) Tropical Savana type
(c) Rainforest type
(d) Tundra type

13. ...... are the coldest months in the Northern part of India.
(a) December and January
(b) January and February
(c) November and December
(d) November and January

14. Where are the dust storms very common during the month of May in Northern India and called as 'Kaal Baisakhi' ?
(a) West Bengal (b) Uttar Pradesh
(c) Punjab (d) Bihar

15. Identify the places where pre-monsoon showers, also called as mango showers, are commonly found which helps in the early ripening of mangoes.
(a) Kerala and Karnataka
(b) Kerala and Tamil Nadu
(c) Tamil Nadu and Andhra Pradesh
(d) Karnataka and Tamil Nadu

16. Which of the following statements is not correct?
(a) The windward side of Western Ghats receives very heavy rainfall, more than 250 cm.
(b) Mawsynram receives the highest average rainfall in the world.
(c) Rainfall in the Ganga Valley decreases from the East to the West.
(d) Maharashtra and parts of Gujarat get scanty rainfall.

17. Identify the area(s) of low precipitation.
(a) Deccan Plateau
(b) East of the Sahyadris
(c) Leh in Jammu and Kashmir
(d) All of the above

18. Complete the given analogy.
Driest place : Leh : : Wettest place : ?
(a) Chennai (b) Mawsynram
(c) Mumbai (d) Pune

19. The summer months experience rising temperature and falling air pressure in which part of India?
(a) Eastern part (b) Western part
(c) Northern part (d) Southern part

20. Which of the following statements defines Continentality?
(a) In Continentality, summers are normal but winters are very cold.
(b) In Continentality, summers are very hot but winters are mild.
(c) In Continentality, summers are very hot and winters are very cold.
(d) None of the above

21. Due to which of the following, the amount of solar energy received varies according to latitude?
(a) Due to pressure and wind system
(b) Due to curvature of the Earth
(c) Due to distance from the sea
(d) Due to ocean currents

22. The air temperature generally decreases from the ....
(a) Equator towards the Poles
(b) Poles towards the Equator
(c) Earth's surface
(d) None of the above

23. Which of the atmospheric conditions govern the climate and associated weather conditions in India?
(a) Pressure and surface winds
(b) Upper air circulation
(c) Western Cyclonic Disturbance and Tropical Cyclones
(d) All of the above

24. What is/are the factor(s) of the climatic controls?
(a) Ocean currents
(b) Relief features
(c) Distance from the sea
(d) All of the above

MCQs 2 Marks Questions

25. Which of the following statements is/are correct?
I. The monsoon winds bind the whole country by providing water to set the agricultural activities in motion.
II. The river valleys which carry this water also unite as a single river valley unit.
Codes
(a) Only I (b) Only II
(c) Both I and II (d) Neither I nor II

26. Arrange the following places according to their distance from the Equator (from minimum to maximum).
I. Leh II. Delhi
III. Thiruvanathapuram IV. Shillong
Codes
(a) I, II, III, IV (b) IV, III, II, I
(c) II, IV, I, III (d) III, I, IV, II

27. Consider the following statements and choose the correct option.
I. The annual precipitation varies from over 400 cm in Meghalaya to less than 10 cm in Ladakh and Western Rajasthan.
II. Most parts of the country receive rainfall from June to September.
Codes
(a) Only I
(b) Only II
(c) Both I and II
(d) Neither I nor II

28. Match the following.

List I (Seasons)	List II (Durations)
A. Cold weather season	1. Mid November-February
B. Hot weather season	2. March-May
C. Advancing monsoon season	3. June-September
D. Retreating/Post monsoon season	4. October-November

Codes
A B C D A B C D
(a) 1 2 3 4 (b) 1 3 2 4
(c) 4 3 1 2 (d) 4 3 2 1

29. There are two statements marked as Assertion (A) and Reason (R). Mark your answer as per the codes given below.
Assertion (A) The Inter Tropical Convergence Zone (ITCZ) is a broad trough of low pressure in equatorial latitudes.
Reason (R) India has mountains to the North, which have an average height of about 6,000 metres.
Codes
(a) Both A and R are true and R is the correct explanation of A
(b) Both A and R are true, but R is not the correct explanation of A
(c) A is true, but R is false
(d) A is false, but R is true

30. Consider the following statements and choose the correct option.

I. The Himalayas prevent the cold winds from Central Asia from entering the sub-continent.

II. The pressure and wind system of any area depend on the latitude and altitude of the place.

III. Ocean currents along with onshore winds affect the climate of the coastal areas.

Codes

(a) Only I (b) I and II

(c) II and III (d) All of these

31. Read the given statements and select which ones are true (T) and which ones are false (F).

I. Parts of Western Coast and North-Eastern India receives rainfall over 400 cm anually.

II. In March, the highest temperature is about 38°C recorded on the Deccan Plateau.

III. In certain places, there is a wide difference between day and night temperatures.

Codes

	I	II	III		I	II	III
(a)	T	T	T	(b)	F	T	F
(c)	T	F	F	(d)	F	F	T

32. Consider the following statements and choose the correct option.

I. The elements of weather and climate are the same, i.e. temperature, atmospheric pressure, wind, humidity and precipitation.

II. The word monsoon is derived from the Arabic word 'mausim' which literally means season.

III. 'Monsoon' refers to the seasonal reversal in the wind direction during a year.

Codes

(a) Only I

(b) I and II

(c) II and III

(d) All of the above

33. On the given map of India, a region is marked as 'A'. This region receives how much annual rainfall?

(a) 20 cm (b) 10 cm

(c) 100 cm (d) 150 cm

Darken your choice with HB Pencil

1. ⓐ ⓑ ⓒ ⓓ	7. ⓐ ⓑ ⓒ ⓓ	13. ⓐ ⓑ ⓒ ⓓ	19. ⓐ ⓑ ⓒ ⓓ	25. ⓐ ⓑ ⓒ ⓓ	31. ⓐ ⓑ ⓒ ⓓ
2. ⓐ ⓑ ⓒ ⓓ	8. ⓐ ⓑ ⓒ ⓓ	14. ⓐ ⓑ ⓒ ⓓ	20. ⓐ ⓑ ⓒ ⓓ	26. ⓐ ⓑ ⓒ ⓓ	32. ⓐ ⓑ ⓒ ⓓ
3. ⓐ ⓑ ⓒ ⓓ	9. ⓐ ⓑ ⓒ ⓓ	15. ⓐ ⓑ ⓒ ⓓ	21. ⓐ ⓑ ⓒ ⓓ	27. ⓐ ⓑ ⓒ ⓓ	33. ⓐ ⓑ ⓒ ⓓ
4. ⓐ ⓑ ⓒ ⓓ	10. ⓐ ⓑ ⓒ ⓓ	16. ⓐ ⓑ ⓒ ⓓ	22. ⓐ ⓑ ⓒ ⓓ	28. ⓐ ⓑ ⓒ ⓓ	
5. ⓐ ⓑ ⓒ ⓓ	11. ⓐ ⓑ ⓒ ⓓ	17. ⓐ ⓑ ⓒ ⓓ	23. ⓐ ⓑ ⓒ ⓓ	29. ⓐ ⓑ ⓒ ⓓ	
6. ⓐ ⓑ ⓒ ⓓ	12. ⓐ ⓑ ⓒ ⓓ	18. ⓐ ⓑ ⓒ ⓓ	24. ⓐ ⓑ ⓒ ⓓ	30. ⓐ ⓑ ⓒ ⓓ	

Chapter 08

Natural Vegetation and Wildlife

MCQs 1 Mark Questions

1. Which among the following has grown naturally without human aid and has been left undistributed by humans for a long time?
   (a) Forests
   (b) Garden
   (c) Natural Vegetation
   (d) All of the above

2. What plays a major role in enhancing the quality of environment?
   (a) Forest
   (b) Temperature
   (c) Weather
   (d) Season

3. How much rainfall is being received by the Tropical Evergreen Forests?
   (a) 100 cm (b) 150 cm
   (c) 200 cm (d) 250 cm

4. Identify the tree(s) which is/are found in Tropical Evergreen Forests.
   (a) Ebony
   (b) Mahogany
   (c) Rosewood
   (d) All of the above

5. Which among the following forests are also called the monsoon forests?
   (a) The Thorn Forests and Scrubs
   (b) Tropical Evergreen Forests
   (c) Tropical Deciduous Forests
   (d) Montane Forests

6. The Dry Deciduous Forests are found in areas having rainfall between …… .
   (a) 100 -70 cm (b) 200-100 cm
   (c) 100-50 cm (d) 150-100 cm

7. Name the forests which are found in Gujarat and Rajasthan.
   (a) Montane Forests
   (b) The Thorn Forests and Scrubs
   (c) Tropical Evergreen Forests
   (d) Montane Forests

8. Silver fir, junipers, pines and birches are the common trees of which type of forests?
   (a) Tropical Deciduous Forests
   (b) Tropical Thorn Forests and Scrubs
   (c) Montane Forests
   (d) Mangrove Forests

9. The common animal found in Montane Forests is ....
   (a) Kashmir Stag (b) Yak
   (c) Snow Leopard (d) All of these

10. Identify the type of vegetation which covers the deltas of the Ganga, the Mahanadi, the Krishna, the Godavari and the Kaveri.
    (a) Mangrove Forests
    (b) Montane Forests
    (c) Tropical Deciduous Forests
    (d) Tropical Thorn Forests and Scrubs

11. Royal Bengal Tiger is the famous animal in which of the following forests?
(a) Tropical Deciduous Forests
(b) Tropical Thorn Forests and Scrubs
(c) Montane Forests
(d) Mangrove Forests

12. The leaves of which tree are used as a cure for eye sores?
(a) Arjun
(b) Babool
(c) Neem
(d) Tulsi

13. Name the tree which has high antibiotic and antibacterial properties.
(a) Neem
(b) Tulsi
(c) Jamun
(d) Sarpagandha

14. Which of the following National Parks is the natural habitat of the Indian lion ?
(a) Gir National Park
(b) Manas National Park
(c) Kaziranga National Park
(d) Bandhavgarh National Park

15. Where are the one horned rhinoceroses found?
(a) Swampy and marshy lands of Meghalaya.
(b) Swampy and marshy lands of Assam.
(c) Swampy and marshy lands of West Bengal.
(d) Both (b) and (c)

16. Complete the given analogy.
Uttarakhand : Jim Corbett National Park : : Kerala : ?
(a) Periyar National Park
(b) Simlipal National Park
(c) Kanha National Park
(d) Chandra Prabha National Park

17. Which among the following options best signifies the type of forests given in the picture?

(a) Tropical Deciduous Forests
(b) Tropical Thorn Forests and Scrubs
(c) Montane Forests
(d) Mangrove Forests

18. Identify the incorrectly matched pair.

	National Parks		Location
(a)	Dudhwa National Park	–	Uttar Pradesh
(b)	Kanha National Park	–	Madhya Pradesh
(c)	Manas National Park	–	Gujarat
(d)	Keoladeo National Park	–	Rajasthan

MCQs 2 Marks Questions

19. Arrange the following types of Montane Forests according to their altitude/elevation (in ascending order).
I. Temperate Forests
II. Alpine Vegetation
III. Wet Temperate Forests

Codes
(a) III, I, II (b) II, III, I
(c) I, II, III (d) III, II, I

20. Consider the following statements and choose the correct option.

I. India has 18 Biosphere Reserves.

II. There are 101 National Parks, 553 Wildlife Sanctuaries and Zoological gardens in India.

Codes

(a) Only I (b) Only II

(c) Both I and II (d) Neither I nor II

21. Match the following.

	List I		List II
A.	Tropical Evergreen Forests	1.	Mahogany
B.	Tropical Deciduous Forests	2.	Teak
C.	Tropical Thorn Forests and Scrubs	3.	Acacias
D.	Montane Forests	4.	Deodar

Codes

	A	B	C	D		A	B	C	D
(a)	1	2	3	4	(b)	4	3	2	1
(c)	2	4	1	3	(d)	3	1	4	2

22. Which of the following pairs is/are not correctly matched?

I. Arjun – The fresh juice of leaves is a cure for earache.

II. Babool – Leaves are used as a cure for eye sores.

III. Sarpagandha – Antibiotic and antibacterial properties.

Codes

(a) Only I (b) Only III

(c) II and III (d) All of these

23. There are two statements marked as Assertion (A) and Reason (R). Mark your answer as per the codes given below.

Assertion (A) The Mangrove Forests are found in coastal areas influenced by tides.

Reason (R) In the Ganga-Brahmaputra delta, Sundari trees are found, which provide durable hard timber.

Codes

(a) Both A and R are true and R is the correct explanation of A

(b) Both A and R are true, but R is not the correct explanation of A

(c) A is true, but R is false

(d) A is false, but R is true

24. Consider the following statements and choose the correct option.

I. India is one of the 18 mega bio-diversity countries in the world.

II. Forests are renewable resources and play a major role in enhancing the quality of environment.

Codes

(a) Only I

(b) Only II

(c) Both I and II

(d) Neither I nor II

25. Consider the following statements associated with the Tropical Evergreen Forests and select which ones are true (T) and which ones are false (F).

I. Tropical Evergreen Forests are also called Tropical Rainforests.

II. These are found in Western Ghats and the island groups of Lakshadweep, Andaman and Nicobar, upper parts of Assam and Tamil Nadu coast.

III. The trees of these forests reach great heights up to 60 metres or even above.

IV. The common animals found in these forests are elephant, monkey, lemur and deer.

Codes

	I	II	III	IV
(a)	T	F	F	F
(b)	F	T	T	F
(c)	T	T	F	F
(d)	T	T	T	T

26. Identify the forests from the following information.

- This type of vegetation is found in the North-Western part of the country, including semi-arid areas of Gujarat, Rajasthan, Madhya Pradesh, Chhattisgarh, Uttar Pradesh and Haryana.
- Acacias, Palms, Cuphorbias and Cacti are the main plant species of these forests.

Codes

(a) Tropical Deciduous Forests
(b) Tropical Thorn Forests and Scrubs
(c) Mangrove Forests
(d) Dry Deciduous Forests

27. There are two statements marked as Assertion (A) and Reason (R). Mark your answer as per the codes given below.

Assertion (A) The Wet Temperate type of forests are found between a height of 1,000-2,000 m.

Reason (R) The juice from ripe Jamun is used to prepare vinegar, which is carminative and diuretic and has digestive properties.

Codes

(a) Both A and R are true and R is the correct explanation of A
(b) Both A and R are true, but R is not the correct explanation of A
(c) A is true, but R is false
(d) A is false, but R is true

28. Identify the National Park, which is marked as 'A' on the given map of India.

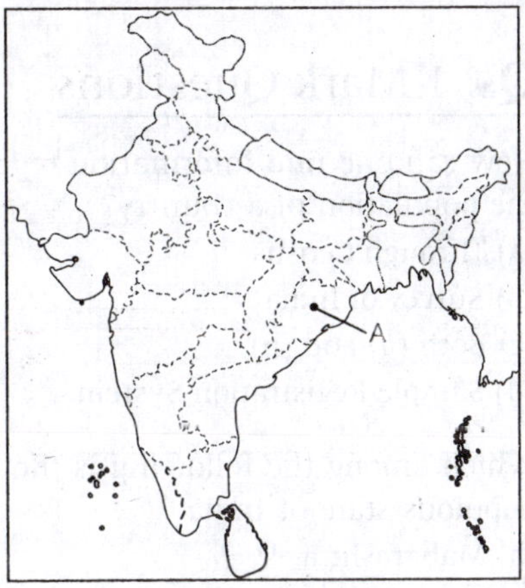

(a) Similipal National Park
(b) Bharatpur National Park
(c) Gir National Park
(d) Ranthambore National Park

Darken your choice with HB Pencil

1.	ⓐ ⓑ ⓒ ⓓ	6.	ⓐ ⓑ ⓒ ⓓ	11.	ⓐ ⓑ ⓒ ⓓ	16.	ⓐ ⓑ ⓒ ⓓ	21.	ⓐ ⓑ ⓒ ⓓ	26.	ⓐ ⓑ ⓒ ⓓ
2.	ⓐ ⓑ ⓒ ⓓ	7.	ⓐ ⓑ ⓒ ⓓ	12.	ⓐ ⓑ ⓒ ⓓ	17.	ⓐ ⓑ ⓒ ⓓ	22.	ⓐ ⓑ ⓒ ⓓ	27.	ⓐ ⓑ ⓒ ⓓ
3.	ⓐ ⓑ ⓒ ⓓ	8.	ⓐ ⓑ ⓒ ⓓ	13.	ⓐ ⓑ ⓒ ⓓ	18.	ⓐ ⓑ ⓒ ⓓ	23.	ⓐ ⓑ ⓒ ⓓ	28.	ⓐ ⓑ ⓒ ⓓ
4.	ⓐ ⓑ ⓒ ⓓ	9.	ⓐ ⓑ ⓒ ⓓ	14.	ⓐ ⓑ ⓒ ⓓ	19.	ⓐ ⓑ ⓒ ⓓ	24.	ⓐ ⓑ ⓒ ⓓ		
5.	ⓐ ⓑ ⓒ ⓓ	10.	ⓐ ⓑ ⓒ ⓓ	15.	ⓐ ⓑ ⓒ ⓓ	20.	ⓐ ⓑ ⓒ ⓓ	25.	ⓐ ⓑ ⓒ ⓓ		

Chapter 09

Population

MCQs 1 Mark Questions

1. How can one find information regarding the population of a country?
   (a) Through Census
   (b) Survey of India
   (c) Both (a) and (b)
   (d) Sample Registration System

2. Which among the following is the most populous state of India ?
   (a) Maharashtra
   (b) Rajasthan
   (c) Bihar
   (d) Uttar Pradesh

3. When did the first complete Census held?
   (a) 1876 (b) 1881
   (c) 1889 (d) 1891

4. Name the largest state of India in terms of area.
   (a) Rajasthan (b) Uttar Pradesh
   (c) Madhya Pradesh (d) Maharashtra

5. When did the State of Jammu and Kashmir was bifurcated into two Union Territories i.e. Jammu and Kashmir and Ladakh ?
   (a) August, 2019
   (b) September, 2019
   (c) October, 2020
   (d) December, 2020

6. Which country has higher average population densities than India?
   (a) Bangladesh (b) Japan
   (c) Pakistan (d) Both (a) and (b)

7. What is the population density of India in the year 2011?
   (a) 382 persons per sq km
   (b) 482 persons per sq km
   (c) 512 persons per sq km
   (d) 1108 persons per sq km

8. Which among the following states of India has the highest population density?
   (a) Nagaland
   (b) Bihar
   (c) Maharashtra
   (d) Uttar Pradesh

9. Identify the State of India which has the lowest population density.
   (a) Assam
   (b) Meghalaya
   (c) Arunachal Pradesh
   (d) Manipur

10. Why the Northern plains and Kerala in the South have high to very high population densities ?
    (a) Flat plains
    (b) Fertile soils
    (c) Abundant rainfall
    (d) All of the above

11. What do you understand by magnitude?
(a) The total population of an area.
(b) The number of persons added each year.
(c) The rate at which the population increases.
(d) The number of females per thousand males.

12. Which of the following play(s) a very significant role in changing the composition and distribution of population?
(a) Death rate (b) Birth rate
(c) Migration (d) All of these

13. The main cause for the high growth of our population is ....
(a) decline of death rate
(b) rise in death rate
(c) decrease in birth rate
(d) None of the above

14. Which movement of the people across regions and territories does not change the size of the population?
(a) Internal (b) External
(c) Death rate (d) Birth rate

15. The size of its adolescent, population constitutes how much of the total population of India?
(a) One-fourth (b) One-fifth
(c) One-sixth (d) One-third

16. Adolescents are generally, grouped in the age group of ....
(a) 7 to 12 years (b) 12 to 19 years
(c) 10 to 19 years (d) 14 to 19 years

17. A large number of adolescent girls in India suffer from which condition(s)?
(a) Anaemia
(b) Scurvy
(c) Rickets
(d) All of the above

18. Name the countries which have higher average population densities than India.
(a) Japan
(b) Bangladesh
(c) China
(d) Both (a) and (b)

19. What is/are the significant feature(s) of National Population Policy (NPP) 2000?
(a) Fulfill the nutritional requirements.
(b) Prevent child marriages.
(c) Educate adolescents about the risks of unprotected sex.
(d) All of the above

20. Identify the incorrect statement.
(a) Birth rate is the number of live births per thousand persons in a year.
(b) In India, most migrations have been from rural to urban areas.
(c) Migration is the movement of people across regions and territories.
(d) None of the above

21. The NPP 2000 provides a policy framework for imparting free and compulsory school education up to ....
(a) 12 years of age
(b) 14 years of age
(c) 10 years of age
(d) 16 years of age

MCQs 2 Marks Questions

22. Consider the following statements and choose the correct option.

I. Migration is an important determinant of population change.

II. Migration does not change the size of the population, but influences the distribution of population within the nation.

Codes

(a) Only I
(b) Only II
(c) Both I and II
(d) Neither I nor II

23. Consider the following statements and choose the incorrect option.

I. The people are important to develop the economy and the society.

II. The people are themselves a resource with poor quality.

III. Human beings are producers and consumers of Earth's resources.

Codes

(a) Only I
(b) Only II
(c) Both II and III
(d) All of the above

24. There are two statements marked as Assertion (A) and Reason (R). Mark your answer as per the codes given below.

Assertion (A) Almost half of India's population lives in just five States.

Reason (R) Rajasthan has only 5.5 per cent of the total population of India.

Codes

(a) Both A and R are true and R is the correct explanation of A
(b) Both A and R are true, but R is not the correct explanation of A
(c) A is true, but R is false
(d) A is false, but R is true

25. Read the passage and answer the following question.

Recognising that the planning of families would improve individual health and welfare, the Government of India initiated a comprehensive Family Planning Programme in 1952. The Family Welfare Programme has sought to promote responsible and planned parenthood on a voluntary basis.

The NPP 2000 provides a policy framework for imparting free and compulsory school education up to ....

(a) 11 years of age (b) 13 years of age
(c) 12 years of age (d) 14 years of age

26. Read the following statements and select which ones are true (T) and which ones are false (F).

I. Natural events like a flood or a tsunami, becomes a 'disaster' only when they affect a crowded village or a town.

II. Telangana became the 29th State of India in June, 2014.

III. Assam and most of the Peninsular states have moderate population densities.

Codes

	I	II	III
(a)	T	F	T
(b)	T	T	F
(c)	T	T	T
(d)	F	T	F

27. Consider the following statements and choose the correct option.

I. The Indian census is the most comprehensive source of demographic, social and economic data.

II. A census is an official enumeration of population done periodically.

III. The most significant feature of the Indian population is the size of its adolescent population.

Codes

(a) Only I (b) I and II

(c) II and III (d) All of these

28. There are two statements marked as Assertion (A) and Reason (R). Mark your answer as per the codes given below.

Assertion (A) In India, most migrations have been from rural to urban areas because of the 'Push' factor in rural areas.

Reason (R) Push factors include poverty and unemployment in rural areas.

Codes

(a) Both A and R are true and R is the correct explanation of A

(b) Both A and R are true, but R is not the correct explanation of A

(c) A is true, but R is false

(d) A is false, but R is true

29. Name the state having moderate population density, which is marked as 'A' on the given map of India.

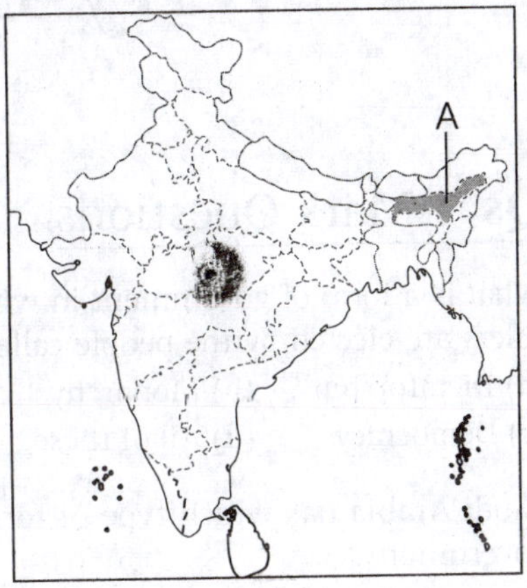

(a) Manipur (b) Nagaland

(c) Assam (d) Meghalaya

Darken your choice with HB Pencil

1.	ⓐ ⓑ ⓒ ⓓ	6.	ⓐ ⓑ ⓒ ⓓ	11.	ⓐ ⓑ ⓒ ⓓ	16.	ⓐ ⓑ ⓒ ⓓ	21.	ⓐ ⓑ ⓒ ⓓ	26.	ⓐ ⓑ ⓒ ⓓ
2.	ⓐ ⓑ ⓒ ⓓ	7.	ⓐ ⓑ ⓒ ⓓ	12.	ⓐ ⓑ ⓒ ⓓ	17.	ⓐ ⓑ ⓒ ⓓ	22.	ⓐ ⓑ ⓒ ⓓ	27.	ⓐ ⓑ ⓒ ⓓ
3.	ⓐ ⓑ ⓒ ⓓ	8.	ⓐ ⓑ ⓒ ⓓ	13.	ⓐ ⓑ ⓒ ⓓ	18.	ⓐ ⓑ ⓒ ⓓ	23.	ⓐ ⓑ ⓒ ⓓ	28.	ⓐ ⓑ ⓒ ⓓ
4.	ⓐ ⓑ ⓒ ⓓ	9.	ⓐ ⓑ ⓒ ⓓ	14.	ⓐ ⓑ ⓒ ⓓ	19.	ⓐ ⓑ ⓒ ⓓ	24.	ⓐ ⓑ ⓒ ⓓ	29.	ⓐ ⓑ ⓒ ⓓ
5.	ⓐ ⓑ ⓒ ⓓ	10.	ⓐ ⓑ ⓒ ⓓ	15.	ⓐ ⓑ ⓒ ⓓ	20.	ⓐ ⓑ ⓒ ⓓ	25.	ⓐ ⓑ ⓒ ⓓ		

Chapter 10

What is Democracy? Why Democracy?

MCQs 1 Mark Questions

1. What is a form of government in which the rulers are elected by the people called?
   (a) Dictatorship (b) Monarchy
   (c) Democracy (d) All of these

2. Saudi Arabia has which type of form of government?
   (a) Monarchy (b) Dictatorship
   (c) Democratic (d) None of these

3. Which of the following features of Democracy is/are responsible to improve the quality of decision-making?
   (a) Democracy is based on consultation and discussion.
   (b) Democratic decision always involves many persons.
   (c) Democratic decisions are taken after discussions and meetings.
   (d) All of the above

4. When did Pervez Musharraf led a military coup in Pakistan ?
   (a) October, 1999
   (b) December, 2000
   (c) November, 2002
   (d) September, 2004

5. What is the Chinese Parliament called?
   (a) National People's Congress
   (b) Chinese Communist Party
   (c) The Community Party of China
   (d) People's Congress

6. How many members (approx) are elected to the National People's Congress from all over China?
   (a) 2500 (b) 3000
   (c) 4000 (d) 5000

7. Since Independence in ……, Mexico holds election after every six years to elect its President.
   (a) 1930 (b) 1940
   (c) 1955 (d) 1965

8. In Saudi Arabia, women did not have the Right to Vote till which year?
   (a) 2015 (b) 2014
   (c) 2010 (d) 2005

9. Which among the following is considered as an accountable form of government?
   (a) Autocratic Government
   (b) Dictator Government
   (c) Democratic Government
   (d) Military Government

10. What kind of oppression did Robert Mugabe give to his people?

(a) Opposition party workers were harassed and their meeting disrupted.

(b) Public protests and demonstrations against the government were declared illegal.

(c) There was a law that limited the Right to Criticise the President.

(d) All of the above

11. When did Zimbabwe attained Independence from white minority rule?

(a) 1970 (b) 1980

(c) 1985 (d) 1987

12. Who among the following was the President of Zimbabwe ?

(a) Robert Mugabe

(b) Pinochet

(c) Parvez Musharraf

(d) Beam Achebe

13. Find the incorrect statement(s) from the given options.

(a) Democracy is based on a fundamental principle of political equality.

(b) Democracy enhances the dignity of citizens.

(c) Democracy leads to corruption, as it is based on electoral competition.

(d) All of the above

14. What does the hidden side of the dictator in the picture depict?

(a) Brutal side of dictator

(b) Sign of wisdom

(c) Courage of the dictator

(d) None of the above

15. What do you understand by the General Election?

(a) Elections that held in all constituencies at the same time.

(b) Elections that held in all constituencies on the same day.

(c) Elections that held in all constituencies within a few days.

(d) All of the above

MCQs 2 Marks Questions

16. Arrange the following statements in chronological order.

I. 'Legal Framework Order' issued by Musharraf

II. Mexico got its Independence

III. Mugabe was removed from office

Codes

(a) II, III, I

(b) I, II, III

(c) III, II, I

(d) II, I, III

17. Consider the following statements and select the correct option.

I. In a Democracy, final decision-making power must rest with those elected by the people.

II. Democracy is a form of government in which the rulers are elected by the people.

Codes

(a) Only I

(b) Only II

(c) Both I and II

(d) Neither I nor II

18. Match the following.

List I	List II
A. PRI	1. Institutional Revolutionary Party
B. National people's	2. Ruling party in China
C. Institutional Revolutionary Party	3. Formed in Mexico in 1930
D. ZANU-PF	4. Party that led the freedom struggle of Zimbabwe

Codes

	A	B	C	D		A	B	C	D
(a)	1	2	3	4	(b)	4	3	2	1
(c)	2	4	1	3	(d)	3	1	4	2

19. Identify the statement(s) associated with the arguments for Democracy.

I. Only in a Democracy, different groups of people can live together peacefully.

II. Democracy is based on the principle of political equality.

III. Democracy requires that the rulers have to attend to the needs of the people.

Codes

(a) Only I

(b) Only II

(c) Only III

(d) All of the above

20. Read the given statements and select which ones are true (T) and which ones are false (F).

I. China's famine of 1958-1961, was the worst recorded famine in the world.

II. A democratic decision involves consultation with and consent of all those people, who are affected by that decision.

III. Democracy provides a method to deal with differences and conflicts.

IV. Democratic government is more accountable form of government.

Codes

	I	II	III	IV
(a)	T	F	T	F
(b)	F	F	T	T
(c)	T	T	F	T
(d)	T	T	T	T

21. Consider the following statements and choose the correct option.

I. A democratic government rules within the limits set by constitutional and citizens rights.

II. In a Democracy, people's will is ascertained by each adult citizen having one vote and each vote has one value.

III. Democracy must be based on a free and fair election, where those currently in power have a fair chance of losing.

Codes

(a) Only I

(b) I and II

(c) II and III

(d) All of the above

22. Identify the personality from the following information.

- He led a military coup in October, 1999. He overthrew the democratically elected government and went on to become the President of the country.
- In 2002, he held a referendum in the country that granted him a five-year extension.

(a) General Pervez Musharraf

(b) Robert Mugabe

(c) Nawaz Sharif

(d) Benazir Bhutto

23. There are two statements marked as Assertion (A) and Reason (R). Mark your answer as per the codes given below.

Assertion (A) In China, elections are held after every five years for electing the country's parliament, called Quanguo Renmin Daibiao Dahui (National People's Congress).

Reason (R) Zimbabwe attained Independence from white minority rule in 1980 and from then the country has been ruled by the party that led the freedom struggle, ZANU-PF.

Codes

(a) Both A and R are true and R is the correct explanation of A

(b) Both A and R are true, but R is not the correct explanation of A

(c) A is true, but R is false

(d) A is false, but R is true

24. Consider the following statements associated with powers of the Prime Minister and select which ones are true (T) and which ones are false (F).

I. The Prime Minister is the head of the government.

II. He coordinates the work of different departments.

III. His decisions are final in case disagreements arise between departments.

IV. He exercises general supervision of different ministries.

Codes

	I	II	III	IV
(a)	T	F	F	F
(b)	F	T	T	F
(c)	T	T	F	F
(d)	T	T	T	T

25. Consider the following statements and select the correct option.

I. India has an integrated Judiciary which means the Supreme Court controls the judicial administration in the country.

II. Sometimes elections are held only for one constituency to fill the vacancy caused by the death or resignation of a member, which is called a By-Election.

III. The Supreme Court and the High Courts have the power to interpret the Constitution of the country.

Codes

(a) Only I (b) I and II

(c) II and III (d) All of these

Darken your choice with HB Pencil

1.	ⓐ ⓑ ⓒ ⓓ	6.	ⓐ ⓑ ⓒ ⓓ	11.	ⓐ ⓑ ⓒ ⓓ	16.	ⓐ ⓑ ⓒ ⓓ	21.	ⓐ ⓑ ⓒ ⓓ
2.	ⓐ ⓑ ⓒ ⓓ	7.	ⓐ ⓑ ⓒ ⓓ	12.	ⓐ ⓑ ⓒ ⓓ	17.	ⓐ ⓑ ⓒ ⓓ	22.	ⓐ ⓑ ⓒ ⓓ
3.	ⓐ ⓑ ⓒ ⓓ	8.	ⓐ ⓑ ⓒ ⓓ	13.	ⓐ ⓑ ⓒ ⓓ	18.	ⓐ ⓑ ⓒ ⓓ	23.	ⓐ ⓑ ⓒ ⓓ
4.	ⓐ ⓑ ⓒ ⓓ	9.	ⓐ ⓑ ⓒ ⓓ	14.	ⓐ ⓑ ⓒ ⓓ	19.	ⓐ ⓑ ⓒ ⓓ	24.	ⓐ ⓑ ⓒ ⓓ
5.	ⓐ ⓑ ⓒ ⓓ	10.	ⓐ ⓑ ⓒ ⓓ	15.	ⓐ ⓑ ⓒ ⓓ	20.	ⓐ ⓑ ⓒ ⓓ	25.	ⓐ ⓑ ⓒ ⓓ

Chapter 11

Constitutional Design and Democratic Rights

MCQs 1 Mark Questions

1. Apartheid was the name of a system of ...... discrimination unique to South Africa.
   (a) racial
   (b) gender
   (c) economic status
   (d) religion

2. Which organisation led the struggle against the policies of segregation in South Africa?
   (a) The African National Congress
   (b) Agang South Africa
   (c) United Democratic Movement
   (d) National Freedom Party

3. In what way(s) did the system of apartheid discriminate among the South Africans?
   (a) It restricted social contacts between the races.
   (b) It segregated public facilities.
   (c) It created race-specific job categories.
   (d) All of the above

4. What is the autobiography written by Nelson Madela called?
   (a) The Story of My Life
   (b) Long Walk to Freedom
   (c) Long Freedom
   (d) None of the above

5. What was the most salient underlying conflict in the making of a democratic Constitution in South Africa?
   (a) Conflict between South Africa and its neighbours
   (b) Conflict between men and women
   (c) Conflict between the white majority and the black minority
   (d) Conflict between the coloured minority and the black majority

6. How many years did it take South Africa to make its Constitution?
   (a) 3 years (b) 2 years
   (c) 6 months (d) 1 year

7. When was the Constitution of India drafted at first?
   (a) 1930 (b) 1931
   (c) 1928 (d) 1929

8. Why do we need a Constitution?
   (a) It generates a degree of trust and coordination that is necessary for different kind of people to live together.
   (b) It specifies how the government will be constituted, who will have the power to take decisions.
   (c) It lays down limits on the powers of the government and tells us what the rights of the citizens.
   (d) All of the above

9. When were elections to the Constituent Assembly held?
   (a) 1945 (b) 1946
   (c) 1944 (d) 1943

10. From which of the following Colonial laws, the Indian Constitution adopted many institutional details and procedures?
    (a) Government of India Act, 1935
    (b) Indian Council Act, 1892
    (c) Charter Act, 1853
    (d) Government of India Act, 1858

11. Who among the following was the Chairman of the Drafting Committee?
    (a) Dr B R Ambedkar
    (b) Motilal Nehru
    (c) Sachidanand Singh
    (d) Jawaharlal Nehru

12. What is a distinct section of a document called?
    (a) Phrase (b) Clause
    (c) Remark (d) Subsection

13. Identify the personality, shown in the picture given below, who was Vice-Chairman of the Constituent Assembly.

    (a) Jagpal Singh (b) HC Mookherjee
    (c) BR Ambedkar (d) KM Munshi

14. What do you mean by Sovereign?
    (a) People have the supreme right to make decisions on internal as well as external matters.
    (b) Wealth is generated socially and should be shared equally by society.
    (c) A form of government where people enjoy equal political rights, elect their rulers and hold them accountable.
    (d) None of the above

15. Who among the following was not a member of Constituent Assembly?
    (a) HC Mookherjee
    (b) Mahatma Gandhi
    (c) Shyama Prasad Mukherjee
    (d) BR Ambedkar

16. What was the reason given by America for imprisoning people at Guantanamo Bay?
    (a) People had been caught spying.
    (b) People were planning to kill the US President.
    (c) People were planning to set up a Communist Government in the USA.
    (d) None of the above

17. Which of these options is correct regarding Saudi Arabian political system?
    (a) The country is ruled by elected government.
    (b) The king cannot select the Legislature as well as the Executive.
    (c) There is freedom of religion.
    (d) Women are subjected to many public restrictions.

18. Kosovo was a province of which of the following countries before its split?
    (a) Albania (b) Afghanistan
    (c) Yugoslavia (d) Egypt

19. What is meant by Rights?
    (a) One's demand to get everything without sharing with others.
    (b) A right is possible when a person makes a claim that is equally possible for others.
    (c) Not possessing any freedoms.
    (d) None of the above

20. Which among the following cannot be challenged in a court?
(a) Directive Principles of State policy
(b) Fundamental Rights
(c) Freedom to choose any profession or business
(d) Right to move freely to any part of the country

21. Under which Fundamental Right has the Parliament enacted a law giving the Right to Information to the citizens?
(a) Right to Freedom of Religion
(b) Right to Freedom of Thought and Expression
(c) Right to Freedom of Equality
(d) Right to Constitutional Remedies

22. What did Dr Ambedkar refer to the 'Right to Constitutional Remedies' as?
(a) The heart and soul of our Constitution
(b) The heart of our Constitution
(c) The soul of our Constitution
(d) None of the above

23. Who among the following is responsible to appoint National Human Right Commission?
(a) The President of India
(b) The Chief Justice of India
(c) The Prime Minister of India
(d) The Vice-President of India

24. Complete the given analogy.
Durgabai Deshmukh : Chairperson of Central Social Welfare Board : : ? : First Education Minister of India
(a) Rajendra Prasad
(b) Abul Kalam Azad
(c) Sarojini Naidu
(d) Somnath Lahiri

25. The image captures the spirit of South Africa. Why it is known as 'Rainbow Nation'?

(a) The people are unified together like colours of rainbow despite of their complexion.
(b) The spirit of South Africa inspired democrats all over the world.
(c) The determination of people helps them to unite and that leads to information of Rainbow Nation.
(d) None of the above

26. Identify the incorrectly matched pair.
(a) Right to Work – Opportunities to everyone to earn livelihood
(b) Right to Privacy – Communication cannot be opened
(c) Right to Health – Medical care during illness
(d) None of the above

MCQs 2 Marks Questions

27. Arrange the following events in chronological order.
I. Nelson Mandela was sentenced to life imprisonment
II. Indian leaders drafted a Constitution of India
III. South Africa became independent

Codes
(a) II, I, III (b) III, II, I
(c) I, II, III (d) II, III, I

28. Consider the following statements and choose the correct option.

I. Fundamental Rights are guaranteed against the actions of the Legislature, the Executive and any other authorities instituted by the government.

II. There can be no law or action that violates the Fundamental Rights.

Codes

(a) Only I
(b) Only II
(c) Both I and II
(d) Neither I nor II

29. Consider the following statements and choose the correct option.

I. A Constitution is not merely a statement of values and philosophy.

II. It is mainly about embodying these values into institutional arrangements.

Codes

(a) Only I
(b) Only II
(c) Both I and II
(d) Neither I nor II

30. Match the following.

	List I		List II
A.	TT Krishnamachari	1.	Founder President of Aadivasi Mahasabha
B.	Jaipal Singh	2.	Member of Drafting Committee
C.	Sardar Patel	3.	Chairman of Constituent Assembly
D.	Dr Rajendra Prasad	4.	Deputy Prime Minister

Codes

	A	B	C	D		A	B	C	D
(a)	1	2	3	4	(b)	4	3	2	1
(c)	2	1	4	3	(d)	3	1	4	2

31. Read the following statements associated with the Constituent Assembly and select which ones are true (T) and which ones are false (F).

I. The Drafting of the Constitution was done by an assembly of elected representatives called the Constituent Assembly.

II. Elections to the Constituent Assembly were held in July, 1946 and its first meeting was held in December, 1946.

III. The Constituent Assembly that wrote the Indian Constitution had 299 members.

Codes

	I	II	III
(a)	T	F	F
(b)	F	T	T
(c)	T	T	F
(d)	T	T	T

32. Consider the following statements and choose the correct option.

I. The Constitution has clear provisions to prevent exploitation of the weaker sections of the society.

II. The Constitution says that the government shall not deny to any person in India equality before the law or the equal protection of the laws.

III. Any section of citizens with a distinct language or culture have a right to conserve it.

Codes

(a) Only I
(b) Only III
(c) II and III
(d) All of these

33. Consider the following statements and choose the correct option.

I. Right to Constitutional Remedies empowers the citizens to move to a Court of Law in case of any denial of the Fundamental Rights.

II. Freedom to practice religion does not mean that a person can do whatever he wants in the name of religion.

Codes

(a) Only I (b) Only II
(c) Both I and II (d) Neither I nor II

34. Identify the Fundamental Right from the following information.

- Under this right, the Constitution prohibits 'traffic in human beings'. Traffic means selling and buying of human beings, usually women, for immoral purposes.
- Under this right, the Constitution prohibits forced labour or begar in any form.

(a) Right against Exploitation
(b) Right to Equality
(c) Cultural and Educational Rights
(d) Right to Freedom

35. Identify the personality from the following information.

- He was the Minister of Industry and Supply in the Interim Government. He was active in Hindu Mahasabha.
- He was the founder President of the Bharatiya Jana Sangh.

(a) Shyama Prasad Mukherjee
(b) Somnath Lahiri
(c) Pt Jawaharlal Nehru
(d) Sardar Patel

36. There are two statements marked as Assertion (A) and Reason (R). Mark your answer as per the codes given below.

Assertion (A) Secularism is based on the idea that the state is concerned only with relations among human beings and not with the relation between human beings and God.

Reason (R) National Human Rights Commission has been set up by law in 1993.

Codes

(a) Both A and R are true and R is the correct explanation of A
(b) Both A and R are true, but R is not the correct explanation of A
(c) A is true, but R is false
(d) A is false, but R is true

Darken your choice with HB Pencil

1. ⓐ ⓑ ⓒ ⓓ	7. ⓐ ⓑ ⓒ ⓓ	13. ⓐ ⓑ ⓒ ⓓ	19. ⓐ ⓑ ⓒ ⓓ	25. ⓐ ⓑ ⓒ ⓓ	31. ⓐ ⓑ ⓒ ⓓ
2. ⓐ ⓑ ⓒ ⓓ	8. ⓐ ⓑ ⓒ ⓓ	14. ⓐ ⓑ ⓒ ⓓ	20. ⓐ ⓑ ⓒ ⓓ	26. ⓐ ⓑ ⓒ ⓓ	32. ⓐ ⓑ ⓒ ⓓ
3. ⓐ ⓑ ⓒ ⓓ	9. ⓐ ⓑ ⓒ ⓓ	15. ⓐ ⓑ ⓒ ⓓ	21. ⓐ ⓑ ⓒ ⓓ	27. ⓐ ⓑ ⓒ ⓓ	33. ⓐ ⓑ ⓒ ⓓ
4. ⓐ ⓑ ⓒ ⓓ	10. ⓐ ⓑ ⓒ ⓓ	16. ⓐ ⓑ ⓒ ⓓ	22. ⓐ ⓑ ⓒ ⓓ	28. ⓐ ⓑ ⓒ ⓓ	34. ⓐ ⓑ ⓒ ⓓ
5. ⓐ ⓑ ⓒ ⓓ	11. ⓐ ⓑ ⓒ ⓓ	17. ⓐ ⓑ ⓒ ⓓ	23. ⓐ ⓑ ⓒ ⓓ	29. ⓐ ⓑ ⓒ ⓓ	35. ⓐ ⓑ ⓒ ⓓ
6. ⓐ ⓑ ⓒ ⓓ	12. ⓐ ⓑ ⓒ ⓓ	18. ⓐ ⓑ ⓒ ⓓ	24. ⓐ ⓑ ⓒ ⓓ	30. ⓐ ⓑ ⓒ ⓓ	36. ⓐ ⓑ ⓒ ⓓ

Chapter 12

Electoral Politics and Working of Institutions

MCQs 1 Mark Questions

1. Since 1982-1987, Haryana was ruled by which political party?
   (a) Congress
   (b) BJP
   (c) Lok Dal
   (d) Janata Dal

2. What is not a sign of democratic elections?
   (a) Everyone should have one vote and every vote should have equal value.
   (b) Elections must be held regularly after every few years.
   (c) It is must that the candidate preferred by the people should get elected.
   (d) None of the above

3. Which among the following is/are the demerit(s) of electoral politics?
   (a) Different political parties and candidates often use dirty tricks.
   (b) The pressure to win electoral fights does not allow to form useful long-term policies.
   (c) Some good people who may wish to serve the country do not enter in electoral competition.
   (d) All of the above

4. What creates a sense of disunity and factionalism?
   (a) Democracy
   (b) Non-democracy
   (c) Political competition
   (d) Absence of political competition

5. What is the tenure of the Lok Sabha?
   (a) 7 years (b) 6 years
   (c) 5 years (d) 4 years

6. .... is an election held for only one constituency, to fill the vacancy caused due to the death or resignation of a member.
   (a) By-election (b) Mid-term election
   (c) General election (d) Assembly election

7. For Lok Sabha elections, the country is divided into how many numbers of constituencies?
   (a) 544 (b) 534
   (c) 543 (d) 541

8. How many seats are reserved for Scheduled Castes (SCs) in Lok Sabha?
   (a) 47 (b) 84
   (c) 78 (d) 56

9. What proportion of seats are reserved in rural and urban local bodies for women candidates?
(a) One-third of the total seats
(b) Two-third of the total seats
(c) Half of the total seats
(d) One-fourth of the total seats

10. Identify the term used for the areas of a country which is divided into different parts for purposes of elections.
(a) Block Constituencies
(b) District Constituencies
(c) Assembly Constituencies
(d) Ward Constituencies

11. Choose the correct statement(s).
(a) At the constituency level, elections take the form of competition among several candidates.
(b) There is no election qualification for candidates for being an MP or MLA.
(c) Every citizen has the Right to Vote regardless of his or her caste, religion or gender.
(d) All of the above

12. Which of the following is not allowed while carrying out election campaign?
(a) Giving money to voters to cast vote for candidates
(b) Using TV channels
(c) Door-to-door canvassing
(d) Contacting voters on phone

13. Campaigns take place for a period of ...... between the announcement of the final list of candidates and the date of polling.
(a) two weeks (b) one week
(c) three weeks (d) one month

14. Identify the roles which is not associated with Election Commission.
(a) The Election Commission conducts all elections for the Parliament and Assemblies.
(b) The Election Commission directs and controls the preparation of electoral roll.
(c) The Election Commission can fix the election dates.
(d) None of the above

15. Who appoints the Chief Election Commissioner of India?
(a) The Chief Justice of India
(b) The Prime Minister of India
(c) The President of India
(d) The Speaker of the Lok Sabha

16. What is meant by 'Office Memorandum'?
(a) Order issued by the Government of India
(b) Memoirs of the leaders of the past
(c) Important defence documents
(d) None of the above

17. When was the Second Backward Class Commission appointed?
(a) 1989 (b) 1979
(c) 1999 (d) 2001

18. Which of the following is/are not the role(s) of the Parliament?
(a) Parliament is the final authority for making laws in any country.
(b) Parliament all over the world can make new laws, change existing laws or abolish existing laws and make new ones in their place.
(c) Parliament make decisions regarding international warfare.
(d) All of the above

19. How many constituencies does Assam have?
    (a) 24
    (b) 14
    (c) 28
    (d) 10

20. For how long can the Rajya Sabha delay a Money Bill?
    (a) 15 days
    (b) 1 month
    (c) 3 months
    (d) 14 days

21. Which among the following statements is/are associated with Political Executive?
    (a) They are elected by the people for a specific period.
    (b) They have more power than the permanent executive.
    (c) They are answerable to the people for all consequences of their decision.
    (d) All of the above

22. Which of the following is not a feature related to the President?
    (a) The President is elected directly by the people.
    (b) A candidate standing for President's post has to get a majority of votes to win the election.
    (c) All International treaties and agreements are made in the name of the President.
    (d) None of the above

23. How can a Judge of the Supreme Court be removed?
    (a) By the Supreme Court itself
    (b) By the Parliament through impeachment
    (c) By the President
    (d) By the Police

24. Complete the given analogy.
    Seats are reserved for the SC in Lok Sabha : 84 : : Seats are reserved for the ST in Lok Sabha : ?
    (a) 57 (b) 37
    (c) 47 (d) 27

25. What does the given picture depict?

    (a) Most of the leaders make many big promises to voters.
    (b) After the elections, political leaders forget their promises.
    (c) People select their representative as per their choice in an election.
    (d) Both (a) and (b)

MCQs 2 Marks Questions

26. Which among the following statements is not correct?
    I. The President is the Supreme Commander of the defence forces of India.
    II. The Prime Minister chairs and takes most of the decision in the Cabinet meetings.
    III. The President supervises the overall functioning of all the political institutions in the country.

    Codes
    (a) Only I (b) Only II
    (c) Only III (d) None of these

27. Arrange the given states (according to seats in Lok Sabha) in ascending order.

I. Maharashtra

II. Andhra Pradesh

III. Karnataka

Codes

(a) II, III, I (b) I, II, III

(c) III, II, I (d) II, I, III

28. Consider the following statements and select the correct option.

I. Independence of the judiciary means that it is not under the control of the Legislature or the Executive.

II. A judge can be removed only by an impeachment motion passed separately by two-thirds members of the two Houses of the Parliament.

Codes

(a) Only I (b) Only II

(c) Both I and II (d) Neither I nor II

29. Read the following statements associated with powers of the Prime Minister and select which ones are true (T) and which ones are false (F).

I. The Prime Minister is the head of the government.

II. He coordinates the work of different departments.

III. His decisions are final in case disagreements arise between departments.

IV. He exercises general supervision of different ministries.

Codes

	I	II	III	IV
(a)	T	F	F	F
(b)	F	T	T	F
(c)	T	T	F	F
(d)	T	T	T	T

30. Consider the following statements and select the correct option.

I. India has an integrated judiciary which means the Supreme Court controls the judicial administration in the country.

II. In many countries of the world, the President is both the head of the state and the head of the government.

III. The Supreme Court and the High Courts have the power to interpret the Constitution of the country.

Codes

(a) Only I

(b) I and II

(c) II and III

(d) All of the above

31. There are two statements marked as Assertion (A) and Reason (R). Mark your answer as per the codes given below.

Assertion (A) Elections should be conducted in a free and fair manner, where people can choose as they really wish.

Reason (R) In India, the poor, illiterate and underprivileged people vote in larger proportion as compared to the rich and privileged sections.

Codes

(a) Both A and R are true and R is the correct explanation of A

(b) Both A and R are true, but R is not the correct explanation of A

(c) A is true, but R is false

(d) A is false, but R is true

32. Which of the following statements is/are not correct?

I. Anyone who can be a voter, can also become a candidate in elections.

II. Regular electoral competition provides incentives to political parties and leaders.

III. It is the responsibility of the government to get the names of all the eligible voters put on the voters' list.

Codes

(a) Only I (b) I and II
(c) II and III (d) All of these

33. Complete the given flow chart.

States	Number of Constituencies
Uttar Pradesh	80
Tamil Nadu	?
West Bengal	42
Madhya Pradesh	29

(a) 39 (b) 37
(c) 35 (d) 42

34. There are two statements marked as Assertion (A) and Reason (R). Mark your answer as per the codes given below.

Assertion (A) The powers and the Independence of the Indian judiciary allow it to act as the guardian of the Fundamental Rights.

Reason (R) The Judges of the Supreme Court and the High Courts are appointed by the President on the advice of the Prime Minister and in consultation with the Chief Justice of the Supreme Court.

Codes

(a) Both A and R are true and R is the correct explanation of A

(b) Both A and R are true, but R is not the correct explanation of A

(c) A is true, but R is false

(d) A is false, but R is true

Darken your choice with HB Pencil

1. ⓐ ⓑ ⓒ ⓓ	7. ⓐ ⓑ ⓒ ⓓ	13. ⓐ ⓑ ⓒ ⓓ	19. ⓐ ⓑ ⓒ ⓓ	25. ⓐ ⓑ ⓒ ⓓ	31. ⓐ ⓑ ⓒ ⓓ
2. ⓐ ⓑ ⓒ ⓓ	8. ⓐ ⓑ ⓒ ⓓ	14. ⓐ ⓑ ⓒ ⓓ	20. ⓐ ⓑ ⓒ ⓓ	26. ⓐ ⓑ ⓒ ⓓ	32. ⓐ ⓑ ⓒ ⓓ
3. ⓐ ⓑ ⓒ ⓓ	9. ⓐ ⓑ ⓒ ⓓ	15. ⓐ ⓑ ⓒ ⓓ	21. ⓐ ⓑ ⓒ ⓓ	27. ⓐ ⓑ ⓒ ⓓ	33. ⓐ ⓑ ⓒ ⓓ
4. ⓐ ⓑ ⓒ ⓓ	10. ⓐ ⓑ ⓒ ⓓ	16. ⓐ ⓑ ⓒ ⓓ	22. ⓐ ⓑ ⓒ ⓓ	28. ⓐ ⓑ ⓒ ⓓ	34. ⓐ ⓑ ⓒ ⓓ
5. ⓐ ⓑ ⓒ ⓓ	11. ⓐ ⓑ ⓒ ⓓ	17. ⓐ ⓑ ⓒ ⓓ	23. ⓐ ⓑ ⓒ ⓓ	29. ⓐ ⓑ ⓒ ⓓ	
6. ⓐ ⓑ ⓒ ⓓ	12. ⓐ ⓑ ⓒ ⓓ	18. ⓐ ⓑ ⓒ ⓓ	24. ⓐ ⓑ ⓒ ⓓ	30. ⓐ ⓑ ⓒ ⓓ	

Chapter

13

The Story of Village Palampur

MCQs 1 Mark Questions

1. What is the main economic activity in village Palampur ?
   (a) Fishing
   (b) Horticulture
   (c) Agriculture
   (d) Manufacturing

2. Which among the following is/are called as fixed capital(s)?
   (a) Generators
   (b) Turbines
   (c) Computers
   (d) All of the above

3. Money in hand is an example of which of the following capitals?
   (a) human capital
   (b) fixed capital
   (c) working capital
   (d) All of the above

4. Every production organised by combining land, labour, physical capital and human capital are known as ....
   (a) factors of production
   (b) physical capital
   (c) working capital
   (d) None of the above

5. What do you mean by Guintha ?
   (a) The type of village house
   (b) The type of hybrid seeds
   (c) The measuring unit of grain
   (d) The measuring unit of land area in the village

6. Identify the correct option.
   (a) In villages across India, farming is the main production activity.
   (b) Apart from farming, the other production activities, referred to as non-farm activities include small manufacturing, transport, shop-keeping, etc.
   (c) There are four requirements (land, labour, capital and skills) for production of goods and services.
   (d) All of the above

7. What does the term Multiple Cropping mean ?
   (a) Cultivation of wheat and rice.
   (b) Cultivation of two crops in alternate rows.
   (c) Cultivating more than one crop on the same field each year.
   (d) Cultivating crops and rearing animals on the same farm.

8. Which among the following is/are the example(s) of rabi crop?
(a) Cotton (b) Millets
(c) Gram (d) Rice

9. When did the Green Revolution take place in India ?
(a) Late 1960s
(b) Mid 1970s
(c) Early 1960s
(d) Late 1970s

10. .... was the first to try out the modern farming method in India.
(a) Farmers of Uttar Pradesh
(b) Farmers of Haryana
(c) Farmers of Punjab
(d) All of the above

11. What is the effect of Green Revolution on soil?
(a) It enhance soil fertility.
(b) It decreases the soil fertility.
(c) It decreases the production.
(d) None of the above

12. From whom, the small farmers borrow money to arrange for the capital in Palampur?
(a) Banks
(b) Co-operative Societies
(c) Village money lenders
(d) Friends and relatives

13. The minimum wages for a farm labourer set by the government is .... per day (March, 2019).
(a) ₹ 300 (b) ₹ 200
(c) ₹ 260 (d) ₹ 350

14. Which of the following statements is not correct about facilities in Palampur?
(a) Palampur has a well-developed road.
(b) Many houses in Palampur have electric connection.
(c) Palampur has a government primary health centre and and a private dispensary.
(d) None of the above

15. Complete the given analogy.
Rabi crop : Wheat : : Kharif crop : ?
(a) Barley
(b) Mustard
(c) Linseed
(d) Rice

16. What does the picture of agriculture farms given below depict?

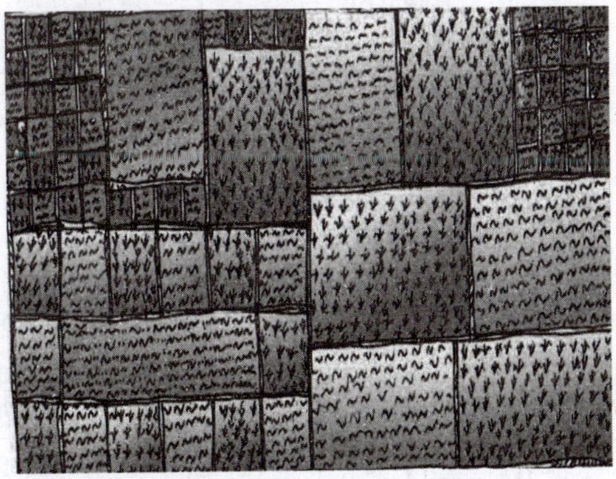

(a) Land of big and middle farmers
(b) Unequal distribution of cultivated land in Palampur
(c) Land distribution of small farmers
(d) Unequal distribution of land in Palampur

MCQs 2 Marks Questions

17. Consider the following statements and choose the correct option.

I. The aim of production is to produce the goods and services that we want.

II. Form labours come either from landless families or families cultivating small plots of land.

Codes

(a) Only I
(b) Only II
(c) Both I and II
(d) Neither I nor II

18. Read the passage and fill in the blanks with appropriate words.
.... is a common activity in many families of Palampur. People feed their buffaloes on various kinds of grass and the jowar and bajra that grows during the .... season.

(a) Dairy, rainy
(b) Farming , winter
(c) Fishing, summer
(d) Dairy, winter

19. Consider the following statements associated with Palampur and select which ones are true (T) and which ones are false (F).

I. In Palampur, about one-third of the 450 families are landless.

II. People of Palampur are engaged in small-scale manufacturing which is carried out at home or in the fields.

III. Traders of Palampur buy various goods from wholesale markets in the cities and sell them in the village.

Codes

	I	II	III		I	II	III
(a)	T	F	F	(b)	F	T	T
(c)	T	T	F	(d)	T	T	T

20. Consider the following statements and choose the correct option.

I. For Palampur, village farming is their main production and the well-being of these people is related to production on the farms.

II. In the rainy season, Kharif farmers grow jowar and bajra followed by the cultivation of potato between October and December.

III. The Green Revolution introduced the Indian farmer to cultivation of wheat and rice using High Yielding Varieties (HYVs) of seeds.

Codes

(a) Only I
(b) I and II
(c) II and III
(d) All of the above

21. There are two statements marked as Assertion (A) and Reason (R). Mark your answer as per the codes given below.

Assertion (A) As compared to the traditional seeds, the HYVs seeds promised to produce much greater amounts of grain on a single plant.

Reason (R) Non-farming activities such as dairy, small-scale manufacturing (e.g. activities of weavers and potters, etc), transport, etc are carried out on a limited scale in Palampur.

Codes

(a) Both A and R are true and R is the correct explanation of A
(b) Both A and R are true, but R is not the correct explanation of A
(c) A is true, but R is false
(d) A is false, but R is true

22. Identify the incorrect statement(s).

I. In Palampur, less than ten per cent people are engaged in the manufacturing sector.

II. Farm labourers will not have any right over the crops grown on the land.

III. Transport services in Palampur include rickshaws, tonga, jeep, tractor, truck drivers, traditional bullock cart and bogey.

Codes

(a) Only I (b) I, II and III

(c) Both II and III (d) All of these

23. Match the following.

List I	List II
A. Land	1. Natural resources
B. Fixed capital	2. Assets
C. Working capital	3. Raw material and money
D. Human capital	4. Knowledge and Enterprises

Codes

	A	B	C	D
(a)	1	2	3	4
(b)	4	3	2	1
(c)	2	4	1	3
(d)	3	1	4	2

24. There are two statements marked as Assertion (A) and Reason (R). Mark your answer as per the codes provided below.

Assertion (A) Only 25 per cent of the people working in Palampur are engaged in activities other than agriculture.

Reason (R) In contrast to the small farmers, the medium and large farmers have their own savings from farming.

Codes

(a) Both A and R are true and R is the correct explanation of A

(b) Both A and R are true, but R is not the correct explanation of A

(c) A is true, but R is false

(d) A is false, but R is true

Darken your choice with HB Pencil

1.	ⓐ ⓑ ⓒ ⓓ	5.	ⓐ ⓑ ⓒ ⓓ	9.	ⓐ ⓑ ⓒ ⓓ	13.	ⓐ ⓑ ⓒ ⓓ	17.	ⓐ ⓑ ⓒ ⓓ	21.	ⓐ ⓑ ⓒ ⓓ
2.	ⓐ ⓑ ⓒ ⓓ	6.	ⓐ ⓑ ⓒ ⓓ	10.	ⓐ ⓑ ⓒ ⓓ	14.	ⓐ ⓑ ⓒ ⓓ	18.	ⓐ ⓑ ⓒ ⓓ	22.	ⓐ ⓑ ⓒ ⓓ
3.	ⓐ ⓑ ⓒ ⓓ	7.	ⓐ ⓑ ⓒ ⓓ	11.	ⓐ ⓑ ⓒ ⓓ	15.	ⓐ ⓑ ⓒ ⓓ	19.	ⓐ ⓑ ⓒ ⓓ	23.	ⓐ ⓑ ⓒ ⓓ
4.	ⓐ ⓑ ⓒ ⓓ	8.	ⓐ ⓑ ⓒ ⓓ	12.	ⓐ ⓑ ⓒ ⓓ	16.	ⓐ ⓑ ⓒ ⓓ	20.	ⓐ ⓑ ⓒ ⓓ	24.	ⓐ ⓑ ⓒ ⓓ

Chapter 14

People as Resources

MCQs 1 Mark Questions

1. Population becomes human capital when there is investment made in the form of ....
   (a) education (b) training
   (c) healthcare (d) All of these

2. People as resources refers to a country's working people in terms of their existing ...... and ....
   (a) abilities, productive skills
   (b) productive skills, abilities
   (c) education, money
   (d) technology, productive skills

3. Investment in human resources through education and medical care can give what level of return in future?
   (a) Minimum (b) Low
   (c) High (d) Average

4. Which of the following countries has invested in human resources due to lack of any natural resources?
   (a) Japan
   (b) South Korea
   (c) New Zealand
   (d) Singapore

5. Sprinkling crops with insecticide is an activity of which sector ?
   (a) Primary sector
   (b) Secondary sector
   (c) Tertiary sector
   (d) Manufacturing sector

6. Identify the example of tertiary sector from the given options.
   (a) Transportation
   (b) Fisheries
   (c) Animal husbandry
   (d) Dairy

7. Find out a non-economic activity from the given options.
   (a) Teacher teaching in school
   (b) Farmer works in his own farm
   (c) Tailor stitching his own clothes
   (d) Restaurants owner cooking for customers

8. Complete the given analogy.
   Primary sector : Poultry farming : : Secondary sector : ?
   (a) Manufacturing
   (b) Fisheries
   (c) Communication
   (d) Sales and services

9. Why are rural women employed in low-paid jobs?

(a) They do not need to work in high-paid jobs.

(b) They lack in education or the necessary skills.

(c) They are not allowed by their families to do high-paid jobs.

(d) They are not aware of the wage structure.

10. What is/are the factor(s) on which the development of country depend ?

(a) Literacy rate

(b) Health of a person

(c) Skill formation of its citizen

(d) All of the above

11. Which among the following enhances by the education?

(a) National income

(b) Cultural richness

(c) Efficiency of governance

(d) All of the above

12. If Kerala has highest literacy rate, then which of the following Indian states has the lowest literacy rate?

(a) Uttarakhand

(b) Jharkhand

(c) Chattisgarh

(d) Bihar

13. Identify the age group of children for which the Sarva Shiksha Abhiyan aims to promote education.

(a) 6 to 10 years (b) 3 to 5 years

(c) 6 to 14 years (d) 7 to 12 years

14. Infant Mortality Rate refers to the death of a child under the age of ....

(a) 1 year (b) 2 years

(c) 3 years (d) 4 years

15. What exists when people who are willing to work at the going wages cannot find jobs?

(a) Unemployment

(b) Seasonal unemployment

(c) Disguised unemployment

(d) Educated unemployment

16. Complete the given analogy.

South Africa : Very high unemployment rate :: India : ?

(a) High unemployment rate

(b) Medium unemployment rate

(c) Low unemployment rate

(d) Zero unemployment rate

17. Which of the following is/are the major determinants of the earning of any individual in the market?

(a) Education

(b) Skills

(c) Both (a) and (b)

(d) Quality of product

MCQs 2 Marks Questions

18. Consider the following statements and select the correct option.

I. Economic activities refer to those activities of humans which are undertaken for a monetary gain or to satisfy his/her wants.

II. Human capital is the stock of skill and productive knowledge embodied in human beings.

Codes

(a) Only I

(b) Only II

(c) Both I and II

(d) Neither I nor II

19. Read the given passage and identify the type of unemployment.

It happens when people are not able to find jobs during some months of the year. People dependent upon agriculture usually face such kind of problem. There are certain busy seasons when sowing, harvesting, weeding and threshing is done. Certain months do not provide much work to the people dependent on agriculture.

(a) Underemployment
(b) Disguised unemployment
(c) Cyclical unemployment
(d) Seasonal unemployment

20. Read the following statements and select which ones are true (T) and which ones are false (F).

I. The unemployment of graduates and post-graduates has increased faster than among matriculates.

II. The health of a person helps him to realise his potential and the ability to fight illness.

III. In the tertiary sector, various new services are now appearing like biotechnology and IT services (call centres).

Codes

	I	II	III		I	II	III
(a)	T	F	F	(b)	F	T	T
(c)	T	T	F	(d)	T	T	T

21. Which among the following statements is/are not correct?

I. Secondary sector includes agriculture forestry, animal husbandry, fishing, poultry farming and mining.

II. A large population can be turned into a productive asset by investment in human capital.

III. Due to historical and cultural reasons, there is a division of labour between men and women in the family.

Codes

(a) Only I
(b) I and II
(c) II and III
(d) All of the above

22. Read the following statements and select the correct option.

Statement (I) Education played an important role for individuals to make better use of economic opportunities.

Statement (II) Women are generally paid less as compared to the men.

Codes

(a) Both statements I and II are incorrect
(b) Both statements I and II are correct
(c) Statement I is correct, but statement II is incorrect
(d) Statement I is incorrect, but statement II is correct

23. Consider the following statements and choose the correct option.

I. Investment in human capital (through education, training, medical care) yields a return just like investment in physical capital.

II. Human capital is superior to other resources like land and physical capital.

Codes

(a) Only I
(b) Only II
(c) Both I and II
(d) Neither I nor II

24. There are two statements marked as Assertion (A) and Reason (R). Mark your answer as per the codes given below.

Assertion (A) Improvement in the health status of the population has been the priority of the country.

Reason (R) The National Policy aimed at improving the accessibility of healthcare, family welfare and nutritional service, especially for the underprivileged segment of the population.

Codes

(a) Both A and R are true and R is the correct explanation of A

(b) Both A and R are true, but R is not the correct explanation of A

(c) A is true, but R is false

(d) A is false, but R is true

25. Match the following.

List I	List II
A. Kerala	1. High number of medical colleges
B. Japan	2. Low Literacy rate
C. Bihar	3. Efficiency of people made the country rich
D. Andhra Pradesh	4. High literacy rate

Codes

	A	B	C	D
(a)	4	2	3	1
(b)	1	2	3	4
(c)	4	3	2	1
(d)	2	3	1	4

26. Identify the type of unemployment from the following information.

This type of unemployment usually happens among family members engaged in agricultural activity. The work requires the services of five people but engages eight people. The contribution made by the three extra people does not add to the contribution made by the five people. If three people are removed the productivity of the field will not decline.

(a) Disguised unemployment

(b) Educated unemployment

(c) Zero unemployment

(d) Cyclical unemployment

Darken your choice with HB Pencil

1.	ⓐ ⓑ ⓒ ⓓ	6.	ⓐ ⓑ ⓒ ⓓ	11.	ⓐ ⓑ ⓒ ⓓ	16.	ⓐ ⓑ ⓒ ⓓ	21.	ⓐ ⓑ ⓒ ⓓ	26.	ⓐ ⓑ ⓒ ⓓ
2.	ⓐ ⓑ ⓒ ⓓ	7.	ⓐ ⓑ ⓒ ⓓ	12.	ⓐ ⓑ ⓒ ⓓ	17.	ⓐ ⓑ ⓒ ⓓ	22.	ⓐ ⓑ ⓒ ⓓ		
3.	ⓐ ⓑ ⓒ ⓓ	8.	ⓐ ⓑ ⓒ ⓓ	13.	ⓐ ⓑ ⓒ ⓓ	18.	ⓐ ⓑ ⓒ ⓓ	23.	ⓐ ⓑ ⓒ ⓓ		
4.	ⓐ ⓑ ⓒ ⓓ	9.	ⓐ ⓑ ⓒ ⓓ	14.	ⓐ ⓑ ⓒ ⓓ	19.	ⓐ ⓑ ⓒ ⓓ	24.	ⓐ ⓑ ⓒ ⓓ		
5.	ⓐ ⓑ ⓒ ⓓ	10.	ⓐ ⓑ ⓒ ⓓ	15.	ⓐ ⓑ ⓒ ⓓ	20.	ⓐ ⓑ ⓒ ⓓ	25.	ⓐ ⓑ ⓒ ⓓ		

Chapter 15

Poverty as a Challenge and Food Security in India

MCQs 1 Mark Questions

1. Which among the following is/are the indicator(s) of poverty?

(a) Lack of shelter
(b) Lack of sanitation
(c) Lack of proper food
(d) All of the above

2. Identify the region(s) which has/have high percentage of people living below poverty line.

(a) Rural (b) Hilly
(c) Urban (d) All of these

3. Who advocated that India would be truly Independent only when the poorest of its people become free of human suffering ?

(a) Mahatma Gandhi
(b) Indira Gandhi
(c) Jawaharlal Nehru
(d) Subhash Chandra Bose

4. Which of the following social indicators is not looked at by social scientists for poverty?

(a) Literacy level
(b) Lack of access to health care
(c) Lack of employment
(d) Lack of access to safe drinking water

5. .... is determined by various options available to different communities in terms of assets, education, job, health, etc.

(a) Social exclusion
(b) Vulnerability
(c) Poverty line
(d) All of the above

6. Name the imaginary line, which is used to estimate poverty in a country.

(a) Social exclusion (b) Poverty line
(c) Vulnerability (d) None of these

7. Which among the following is/are determined for estimating the poverty line?

(a) Clothing
(b) Educational requirement
(c) Medical requirement
(d) All of the above

8. What was the reason behind the higher level of the calorie requirement in the rural areas ?

(a) People do not enjoy as much as people in the urban areas.
(b) Food items are expensive.
(c) People are engaged in mental work.
(d) people are engaged in physical labour.

9. What is the accepted average calorie requirement in urban areas in India?
(a) 2100 calories (b) 2700 calories
(c) 1500 calories (d) 2400 calories

10. The organisation which carries out survey for determining the poverty line is ....
(a) NSSO
(b) CSO
(c) Planning Commission
(d) None of the above

11. Identify the social group(s) which is/are vulnerable to poverty.
(a) Scheduled Caste
(b) Urban casual labour
(c) Rural agricultural households
(d) All of the above

12. Which two states of India continue to be the poorest states?
(a) Odisha and Bihar
(b) Uttar Pradesh and Jharkhand
(c) Madhya Pradesh and Maharashtra
(d) Jharkhand and Rajasthan

13. Look at the picture given below and choose the title that closely relates to the given picture.

(a) Self- sufficiency in food grains
(b) Fair price shop
(c) Massive starvation and food insecurity
(d) Types of hunger

14. What is not the major cause of income inequality in India?
(a) Unequal distribution of land
(b) Lack of fertile land
(c) Gap between the rich and the poor
(d) Increase in population

15. When did the Prime Minister Rojgar Yojana (PMRY) introduced?
(a) 1992 (b) 1993
(c) 1999 (d) 2002

16. What do you understand by food security ?
(a) Availability of food
(b) Accessibility of food
(c) Affordability of food
(d) All of the above

17. Which of the following implies that an individual has enough money to buy sufficient, safe and nutritious food to meet one's dietary needs?
(a) Availability of food (b) Accessibility
(c) Affordability (d) All of these

18. The most devastating famine that occurred in India was the famine of .... in 1943.
(a) Maharashtra (b) Rajasthan
(c) Bihar (d) Bengal

19. What do you mean by chronic hunger?
(a) Low income
(b) Inadequate quantity of food
(c) Inadequate quality of food
(d) All of the above

20. Identify the main purpose(s) of a Buffer Stock Scheme.
(a) To solve the problem of shortage of food.
(b) To support the farmers.
(c) To create the stock for a profit.
(d) All of the above

21. Minimum Support Price is announced by the government to provide incentives to whom?
(a) Farmers
(b) Middlemen
(c) Government officials
(d) None of the above

22. Which of the following statements is not correct about the Public Distribution System (PDS)?
(a) The PDS dealers divert the grain to open market to get a better margin.
(b) They sell poor quality grains at ration shops.
(c) They open shops irregularly.
(d) None of the above

23. Name the scheme(s) which was/were initiated for the poor in all areas.
(a) Antyodaya Anna Yojana (AAY)
(b) Revamped Public Distribution System (RPDS)
(c) Targeted Public Distribution System (TPDS)
(d) All of the above

24. In which state 94 percent ration shops are run by cooperatives?
(a) Andhra Pradesh
(b) Tamil Nadu
(c) Odisha
(d) Bihar

25. On what factor(s) do calorie needs vary for a person?
(a) Age
(b) Sex
(c) Type of work
(d) All of the above

26. Complete the given analogy with suitable code.

2400 calories per person per day : Rural areas : : ? : Urban areas
(a) 2100 calories per person per day
(b) 2200 calories per person per day
(c) 2300 calories per person per day
(d) 2600 calories per person per day

27. Look at the picture given below and choose the suitable title that relates to the given picture.

(a) Buffer stock
(b) Food Corporation of India
(c) MSP
(d) Rationing

MCQs 2 Marks Questions

28. Arrange the following in correct sequence according to their launching period.

I. Prime Minister Rojgar Yojana
II. Rural Employment
III. Antyodaya Anna Yojana

Codes
(a) I, II, III
(b) III, II, I
(c) II, III, I
(d) III, I, II

29. Read the passage and answer the following question.

Sivaraman lives in a small village near Karur town in Tamil Nadu. Karur is famous for its handloom and powerloom fabrics. There are a 100 families in the village. Sivaraman an Aryunthathiyar (cobbler) by caste, now works as an agricultural labourer for ₹ 160 per day. But that's only for five to six months in a year. At other times, he does odd jobs in the town.

Why did Sivaraman need to do odd jobs in the town apart from agriculture?

(a) Agriculture only provides seasonal work
(b) Physical weakness
(c) Lack of skills to work in agriculture
(d) Aryunthathiyar caste is not allowed to work in agriculture for entire year.

30. Read the given statements and select which ones are true (T) and which ones are false (F).

I. Seasonal hunger is related to cycles of food growing and harvesting.
II. Poor people suffer from chronic hunger because of their very low income and in turn inability to buy food even for survival.
III. Food security refers to availability, accessibility and affordability of food to all people at all times.
IV. Ration shops are also known as Fair Price Shops.

Codes

	I	II	III	IV
(a)	F	T	F	T
(b)	T	T	F	F
(c)	F	T	T	F
(d)	T	T	T	T

31. Match the following.

	List I (Programmes)		**List II** (Year of introduced)
A.	Public Distribution System	1.	1992
B.	Targeted Public Distribution System	2.	1997
C.	Antyodaya Anna Yojana	3.	2000
D.	National Food Security Act	4.	2013

Codes

	A	B	C	D		A	B	C	D
(a)	1	2	3	4	(b)	4	3	2	1
(c)	2	4	1	3	(d)	3	1	4	2

32. Read the following passage and identify the scheme.

The scheme was launched in December, 2000. Under this scheme, 1 crore of the poorest among the BPL families covered under the Targeted Public Distribution System were identified. 25 kilograms of foodgrains were made available to each eligible family at a highly subsidised rate of ₹ 2 per kg for wheat and ₹ 3 per kg for rice.

(a) Antyodaya Anna Yojana (AAY)
(b) Public Distribution System
(c) Annapurna Scheme
(d) None of the above

33. Which among the following is/are not correct?

I. Surveys for determining poverty line are carried out by the National Sample Survey Organisation (NSSO).
II. Buffer Stock is the stock of foodgrains (wheat and rice) procured by private sector.

III. The main objective of the food for Work Programme is generation of supplementary wage employment.

Codes

(a) Only I (b) I and III
(c) Only II (d) All of these

34. Read the following statements and select the correct option.

Statement (I) Food Corporation of India (FCI) was set-up under the Food Corporation's Act 1964.

Statement (II) The food Produced by the FCI is distributed through government regulated ration shops among the poorer section of the society.

Codes

(a) Both statements I and II are incorrect
(b) Both statements I and II are correct
(c) Statement I is correct, but statement II is incorrect
(d) Statement I is incorrect, but statement II is correct

35. Match the following.

List I (Programme)	List II (Year of introduced)
A. National Sample Survey Organisation	1. 1950
B. PM Rojgar Yojana	2. 1993
C. Rural Employment Generation Programme	3. 1995
D. Swarna Jayanti Gram Swarozgar Yojana	4. 1999

Codes

	A	B	C	D
(a)	1	2	3	4
(b)	4	3	2	1
(c)	2	4	1	3
(d)	3	1	4	2

Darken your choice with HB Pencil

1. ⓐ ⓑ ⓒ ⓓ	7. ⓐ ⓑ ⓒ ⓓ	13. ⓐ ⓑ ⓒ ⓓ	19. ⓐ ⓑ ⓒ ⓓ	25. ⓐ ⓑ ⓒ ⓓ	31. ⓐ ⓑ ⓒ ⓓ
2. ⓐ ⓑ ⓒ ⓓ	8. ⓐ ⓑ ⓒ ⓓ	14. ⓐ ⓑ ⓒ ⓓ	20. ⓐ ⓑ ⓒ ⓓ	26. ⓐ ⓑ ⓒ ⓓ	32. ⓐ ⓑ ⓒ ⓓ
3. ⓐ ⓑ ⓒ ⓓ	9. ⓐ ⓑ ⓒ ⓓ	15. ⓐ ⓑ ⓒ ⓓ	21. ⓐ ⓑ ⓒ ⓓ	27. ⓐ ⓑ ⓒ ⓓ	33. ⓐ ⓑ ⓒ ⓓ
4. ⓐ ⓑ ⓒ ⓓ	10. ⓐ ⓑ ⓒ ⓓ	16. ⓐ ⓑ ⓒ ⓓ	22. ⓐ ⓑ ⓒ ⓓ	28. ⓐ ⓑ ⓒ ⓓ	34. ⓐ ⓑ ⓒ ⓓ
5. ⓐ ⓑ ⓒ ⓓ	11. ⓐ ⓑ ⓒ ⓓ	17. ⓐ ⓑ ⓒ ⓓ	23. ⓐ ⓑ ⓒ ⓓ	29. ⓐ ⓑ ⓒ ⓓ	35. ⓐ ⓑ ⓒ ⓓ
6. ⓐ ⓑ ⓒ ⓓ	12. ⓐ ⓑ ⓒ ⓓ	18. ⓐ ⓑ ⓒ ⓓ	24. ⓐ ⓑ ⓒ ⓓ	30. ⓐ ⓑ ⓒ ⓓ	

Practice Sets

1-3

Practice Set 01

Time : 60 Mins.

Max. Marks : 60

General Instructions

1. This question paper contains 50 questions.
2. All questions are compulsory. There is no negative marking.
3. Q. No. 1 to 40 are of 1 mark each and Q. No. 41 to 50 are of 2 marks each.
4. Use HB pencil / Blue ball point pen to mark your choice of answer by darkening the circles on the OMR Sheet.

MCQs 1 Mark Questions

1. Identify which Estates in France demanded that each member of an Estate would have one vote.

(a) First Estate
(b) Second Estate
(c) Third Estate
(d) None of the above

2. What was/were the demand(s) made by the workers at St. Petersburg who went on strike?

(a) Reduction in working hours
(b) Increase in wages
(c) Improvement in working conditions
(d) All of the above

3. The 'Greens' who controlled most of the Russian Empire during 1918 and 1919 were known as ....

(a) Menshevik Party
(b) Pro-Tsarists
(c) Socialist Revolutionaries
(d) Bolsheviks

4. Why was the Weimar Republic called 'November Criminals'?

(a) They signed armistice agreement and conceded Germany to Allies.
(b) They crushed Spartacists with the help of free Corps.
(c) They misused Article 48.
(d) They secured loans from USA.

5. When was Hitler offered a Chancellorship of Germany, the highest position in the Cabinet of Ministers by the President?

(a) 30th January, 1931
(b) 30th January, 1932
(c) 30th January, 1933
(d) 28th February, 1932

6. The word 'scientific forestry' best signifies which among the following?

(a) System whereby the local farmers were allowed to cultivate temporarily within a plantation.
(b) System of cutting old trees and planting new ones.
(c) Division of forests into three categories.
(d) Disappearance of forests.

7. Who was the leader of the forest communities who rebelled against the British from Chota Nagpur?

(a) Birsa Munda
(b) Siddhu
(c) Kanu Sanyal
(d) Alluri Sitarama Raju

8. What is the meaning of this picture of 1790?

(a) The fat reducing press symbolises exploitation.
(b) The fat reducing press symbolises justice.
(c) The Reign of Terror gives justice.
(d) None of the above

9. What do you understand by the term pastoral nomads?
(a) The villagers who moved from one place to another.
(b) The people who do not have a permanent place to live in.
(c) The herdsman who moved from one place to another looking for pastures for their herd.
(d) None of the above

10. The .... of Maasai society wear traditional deep red 'shukas', brightly beaded jewellery and steel tipped spears.
(a) warriors (b) elders
(c) rulers (d) villagers

11. Identify the incorrectly matched pair about India.
(a) Area of India – 2.32 million sq km
(b) India has land boundary – 15200 km
(c) North to South Distance – 3214 km
(d) Standard Meridian of India – 82°30′ E

12. How has/have the opening of the Suez Canal helped India?
(a) It is a tourist attraction spot and so, the tourism industry of India has flourished.
(b) The distance between India and Europe has been reduced by 7000 km.
(c) Both (a) and (b)
(d) None of the above

13. Complete the given analogy.
Anai Mudi : Highest peak of Western Ghats : : ? : Highest peak of the Eastern Ghats
(a) Mahendragiri
(b) Doddabetta
(c) Namcha Barwa
(d) Dhaulagiri

14. The part of the Himalayas lying between Satluj and Kali rivers is known as ....
(a) Kumaon Himalayas
(b) Assam Himalayas
(c) Punjab Himalayas
(d) Himachal Himalayas

15. Identify the correct order of the given rivers as per their length (in descending order).
(a) The Ganga, Godavari, Krishna, Kaveri
(b) Krishna, Kaveri, The Ganga, Godavari
(c) Kaveri, The Ganga, Krishna, Godavari
(d) Godavari, Kaveri, The Ganga, Krishna

16. In which district of Madhya Pradesh, the Tapi rises in the Satpura ranges?
(a) Nagada
(b) Vidisha
(c) Betul
(d) Ujjain

17. Which areas experience less contrasts in temperature conditions?
(a) Coastal areas
(b) Plains
(c) Hilly areas
(d) Plateau region

18. Mawsynram in the Southern ranges of which hills receive the highest average rainfall in India?
(a) Naga Hills
(b) Mizo Hills
(c) Khasi Hills
(d) Shevaroy Hills

19. Identify the country which is one of the 12 mega bio-diversity countries of the world.
(a) Japan
(b) India
(c) Thailand
(d) China

20. What does the given picture depict?

(a) Fake promises of the politician
(b) Contribution of political leaders
(c) 75 years of Independence
(d) None of the above

21. After the emergence of the new democratic South Africa, what did the black leaders appeal to fellow blacks?
(a) Forgive the whites for the atrocities they had committed
(b) To take revenge on the whites
(c) The whites must leave the country
(d) None of the above

22. Who among the following was not a member of Constituent Assembly?
(a) Rajendra Prasad
(b) KM Munshi
(c) BR Ambedkar
(d) Mahatma Gandhi

23. Choose the correct statement(s).
(a) Rights are necessary for the substenance of a democracy.
(b) In a democracy, every citizen has the Right to Vote and the Right to be Elected to Government.
(c) Rights protect minorities from the oppression of majority.
(d) All of the above

24. What creates a sense of disunity and 'factionalism'?
(a) Democracy
(b) Non-Democracy
(c) Political competition
(d) Extreme Political Competition

25. Name the state which has highest number of constituencies.
(a) Uttar Pradesh (b) Maharashtra
(c) West Bengal (d) Rajasthan

26. Which of the following is/are not correct about the functions of the Judiciary?
(a) Every law passed by the Parliament needs approval of the Supreme Court.
(b) Judiciary can strike down a law if it goes against the spirit of the Constitution.
(c) Judiciary is independent of the executive.
(d) All of the above

27. When did the Government of India appoint the Second Backward Classes Commission?
(a) 1976 (b) 1979
(c) 1964 (d) 1975

28. Which of these is not a provision under the Culture and Educational Right in India?

(a) Every cultural group has the right to protect its language and culture.

(b) Admissions can be denied on the basis of religion and culture in government aided educational organisations set up by cultural groups.

(c) All minority groups have the right to establish educational institutions of their choice.

(d) None of the above

29. Identify the fixed capital from the given options.

(a) Tools and machines

(b) Fertilisers and pesticides

(c) Soil

(d) Seeds

30. Which of the following statements is incorrect about small-scale manufacturing in villages?

(a) Farmers engage in it to supplement their income.

(b) Farmers take help of their family members.

(c) The production is done mostly at home.

(d) Farmers produce crop for their own use.

31. In the given picture, identify the Kharif crop.

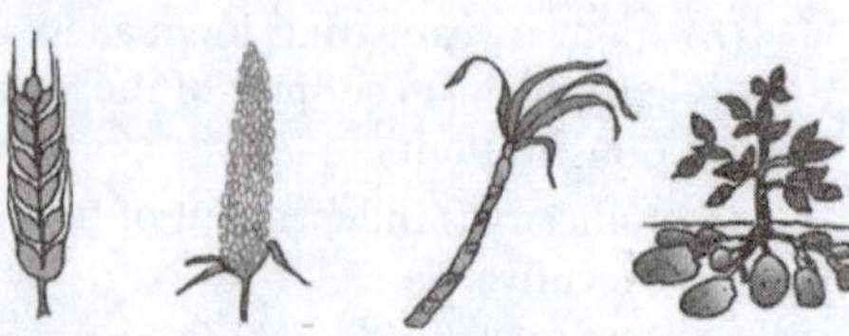

(a) Wheat (b) Bajra (c) Sugarcane (d) Potato

32. The excess population is considered as a burden for an economy but they can become human capital if there is an investment made in the form of ....

(a) education and health

(b) hospitals and schools

(c) education, training and medical care

(d) None of the above

33. What are the terms in which Vulnerability is determined by the options available to different communities for finding an alternative living ?

(a) Assets

(b) Education

(c) Health

(d) All of the above

34. Which organisation carries out survey for determining the poverty line?

(a) NSSO

(b) CSO

(c) Planning Commission

(d) Both (b) and (c)

35. Identify which is not the major cause of income inequality in India.

(a) Unequal distribution of land

(b) Lack of fertile land

(c) Gap between the rich and the poor

(d) Increase in population

36. What is the reason behind Minimum Support Price (MSP) announced by the government ?

(a) To provide incentives to farmers for raising production.

(b) To provide incentives to traders to earn maximum profit from farmers.

(c) To provide incentives to moneylenders to lend maximum to farmers.

(d) None of the above

37. In which of the following states do we find the largest number of food insecurity among people?

(a) Bihar, Jharkhand and Odisha

(b) Bihar, Jharkhand and Gujarat

(c) Bihar, Madhya Pradesh and Tamil Nadu

(d) Bihar, Chhattisgarh and Karnataka

38. Identify the name of the river which originates from the Western Ghats near Mahabaleshwar.
(a) Kaveri
(b) Mahanadi
(c) Krishna
(d) Narmada

39. Which term is associated with Parliamentary democracy in most of the countries?
(a) Cabinet form of government
(b) Legislative system
(c) Majority form of government
(d) Single executive system

40. .... is the stock of skill and productive knowledge embodied in human beings.
(a) Unemployment
(b) Human Capital
(c) National Income
(d) Human Resources

MCQs 2 Marks Questions

41. Identify the National Park marked as 'A' on the physical map of India.

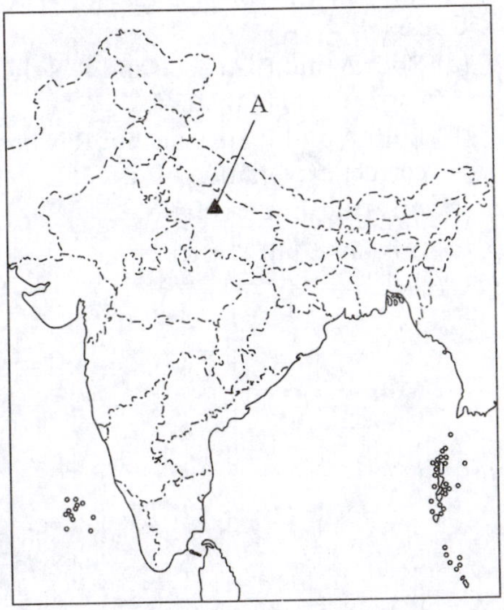

(a) Dudhwa National Park
(b) Bandipur National Park
(c) Simlipal National Park
(d) Jim Corbett National Park

Direction (Q 42 and Q 43) Read the passage and answer the following questions.

Yamuna flows parallel to the Ganga and as a right bank tributary meets the Ganga at Allahabad. The Ghaghara, the Gandak and the Kosi rise in the Nepal Himalaya. They are the rivers, which flood parts of the Northern plains every year, causing widespread damage to life and property, whereas, they enrich the soil for agricultural use.

42. Name the place from where the river Yamuna rises.
(a) Yamunotri Glacier
(b) Gangotri Glacier
(c) Tibet
(d) The Satpura Range

43. Identify the tributary of the River Yamuna.
(a) Chambal
(b) Betwa
(c) Tapi
(d) Both (a) and (b)

44. Match the following.

	List I	List II
A.	Louis XVl ascended the thrown of France	1. 1774
B.	Monarchy abolished in France	2. 1792
C.	Napoleon was defeated in Battle of Waterloo	3. 1915
D.	Women in France won the Right to Vote	4. 1946

Codes

	A	B	C	D
(a)	1	2	3	4
(b)	4	3	2	1
(c)	2	1	4	3
(d)	3	4	1	2

45. Arrange the following in descending order according to their height.

I. Mt Everest
II. Kanchenjunga
III. Nanga Parbat
IV. Nanda Devi

Codes

(a) I, II, III, IV
(b) IV, III, II, I
(c) II, I, IV, III
(d) III, IV, I, II

46. Identify the personality from the given information.

- He believed that to free themselves from capitalist exploitation, workers had to construct a radically socialist society where all property was socially controlled. This would be a communist society.
- He was convinced that workers would triumph in their conflict with capitalists. A communist society was the natural society of the future.

(a) Robert Owen
(b) Louis Blanc
(c) Karl Marx
(d) Friedrich Engels

47. Consider the following statements.

I. In many parts of India and across the world, forest communities rebelled against the changes that were being imposed on them.
II. Bastar is located in the Southernmost part of Chhattisgarh and borders Andhra Pradesh, Odisha and Maharashtra.
III. Java in Indonesia is where the Dutch started forest management.

Which of the following statements is/are correct?

(a) Only I
(b) Both I and II
(c) Only III
(d) All of the above

48. There are two statements marked as Assertion (A) and Reason (R). Mark your answer as per the codes given below.

Assertion (A) All the villages in India do not have a high level of irrigation as in Palampur.

Reason (R) To increase production from the same piece of land, farmers do multiple cropping.

Codes

(a) Both A and R are true and R is the correct explanation of A
(b) Both A and R are true, but R is not the correct explanation of A
(c) A is true, but R is false
(d) A is false, but R is true

49. Read the given statements and select which ones are true (T) and which ones are false (F).

I. In urban areas, casual construction workers suffer from seasonal hunger when they do not get work.

II. A famine is characterised by widespread deaths due to starvation and epidemics.

III. The cooperative societies set-up shops to sell low priced goods to poor people.

IV. Generally, the poor section of the society faces the problem of food security.

Codes

	I	II	III	IV
(a)	T	T	T	T
(b)	T	T	T	F
(c)	T	F	T	F
(d)	F	F	T	T

50. There are two statements marked as Assertion (A) and Reason (R). Mark your answer as per the codes given below.

Assertion (A) Political competition takes place when different political parties compete to gain the confidence and the vote of voters.

Reason (R) Regular electoral competition provides incentives to political parties and leaders.
If they can satisfy the voters with their work, they will be able to win again.

Codes

(a) Both A and R are true and R is the correct explanation of A

(b) Both A and R are true, but R is not the correct explanation of A

(c) A is true, but R is false

(d) A is false, but R is true

Darken your choice with HB Pencil

1.	a	b	c	d	11.	a	b	c	d	21.	a	b	c	d	31.	a	b	c	d	41.	a	b	c	d
2.	a	b	c	d	12.	a	b	c	d	22.	a	b	c	d	32.	a	b	c	d	42.	a	b	c	d
3.	a	b	c	d	13.	a	b	c	d	23.	a	b	c	d	33.	a	b	c	d	43.	a	b	c	d
4.	a	b	c	d	14.	a	b	c	d	24.	a	b	c	d	34.	a	b	c	d	44.	a	b	c	d
5.	a	b	c	d	15.	a	b	c	d	25.	a	b	c	d	35.	a	b	c	d	45.	a	b	c	d
6.	a	b	c	d	16.	a	b	c	d	26.	a	b	c	d	36.	a	b	c	d	46.	a	b	c	d
7.	a	b	c	d	17.	a	b	c	d	27.	a	b	c	d	37.	a	b	c	d	47.	a	b	c	d
8.	a	b	c	d	18.	a	b	c	d	28.	a	b	c	d	38.	a	b	c	d	48.	a	b	c	d
9.	a	b	c	d	19.	a	b	c	d	29.	a	b	c	d	39.	a	b	c	d	49.	a	b	c	d
10.	a	b	c	d	20.	a	b	c	d	30.	a	b	c	d	40.	a	b	c	d	50.	a	b	c	d

Practice Set 02

Time : 60 Mins. Max. Marks : 60

General Instructions

1. This question paper contains 50 questions.
2. All questions are compulsory. There is no negative marking.
3. Q. No. 1 to 40 are of 1 mark each and Q. No. 41 to 50 are of 2 marks each.
4. Use HB pencil / Blue ball point pen to mark your choice of answer by darkening the circles on the OMR Sheet.

MCQs 1 Mark Questions

1. What is the right to seek the enforcement of all Fundamental Rights called?
(a) Right against Exploitation
(b) Right to Freedom
(c) Right to Constitutional Remedies
(d) Cultural and Educational Rights

2. Name the area(s) in India which has a low level of irrigation.
(a) Deccan Plateau
(b) Coastal Regions
(c) Riverine Plains
(d) Both (a) and (b)

3. What is the reason for conducting elections? Identify the incorrect statement from the given options.
(a) Elections enable people to judge the performance of the government.
(b) People elect the representatives of their choice in an election.
(c) Elections enable people to evaluate the performance of the judiciary.
(d) Elections enable people to indicate which policies they prefer.

4. How democracy improves the quality of decision-making ?
(a) Decisions are taken by educated people
(b) Decisions are taken by consultation and discussion.
(c) Decisions are taken over a long period of time.
(d) All decisions are approved by judiciary.

5. Why do the farmers of Palampur follow multiple cropping?
(a) The water consumption is less in this method.
(b) This method consumes less chemical fertilisers.
(c) This method doesn't require fertile soils.
(d) This method is the most common way of increasing production.

6. Which of the options given below is applicable to the principle of Universal Adult Franchise?
(a) Only rich and educated can vote.
(b) Only men can vote.
(c) All citizens aged 18 and above can vote.
(d) Only employed people can vote.

7. The scheme for the establishment of residential schools to impart education to talented children from rural areas is ....
(a) Kendriya Vidyalaya
(b) Navodaya Vidyalaya
(c) Sarvodaya Vidyalaya
(d) None of the above

8. Which crop registered the largest increase in production as a result of Green Revolution?
(a) Wheat (b) Rice
(c) Maize (d) None of these

9. When was National Rural Employment Guarantee Act passed?
(a) September, 2005
(b) August, 2004
(c) May, 2009
(d) None of the above

10. What do moneybags signify here?

(a) Money is the real strength in democracy
(b) It helps political party to win in the election
(c) Both (a) and (b)
(d) None of the above

11. Which of the following is/are correct so far as powers of the Parliament are concerned, apart from making laws?
(a) Exercising control over the government
(b) Controlling finance of the country
(c) Serving as the highest forum of discussion and debate
(d) All of the above

12. If a person in rural areas cannot find jobs during some months of the year, what type of employment is this called?
(a) Structural unemployment
(b) Cyclical unemployment
(c) Seasonal unemployment
(d) None of the above

13. When there is investment made in the form of education, training and medical care, the population becomes ....
(a) Working capital
(b) Human capital
(c) Fixed capital
(d) Capital growth

14. What has reduced India's distance from Europe by 7000 km?
(a) Suez Canal
(b) Panama Canal
(c) Indira Gandhi Canal
(d) Buckingham Canal

15. Why did people react strongly to the Mandal Commission Report?
(a) It left out many backward communities.
(b) It affected thousands of job opportunities.
(c) Some high castes wanted to be included in it.
(d) Both (a) and (c)

16. Which among the following is not a feature of the Indian Constitution?
(a) Double citizenship
(b) Parliamentary form of government
(c) Federal form of government
(d) A written Constitution

17. Who among the following was the President of the Indian Constituent Assembly?
(a) Motilal Nehru
(b) Dr Rajendra Prasad
(c) Sarojini Naidu
(d) BR Ambedkar

18. What was the reason given by America for imprisoning people at Guantanamo Bay?
(a) They had been caught spying.
(b) They were planning to kill the US President.
(c) They were planning to set up a Communist Government in USA.
(d) America considered them as enemies and linked them to the attack on New York on 11th September, 2001.

19. Identify the crop which is grown in the rainy season.
(a) Jowar and bajra (b) Wheat
(c) Soyabean (d) Rice

20. Choose the incorrect reason for the poverty alleviation programme in India.
(a) Lack of proper implementation
(b) Lack of right targeting
(c) Corruption at the highest level
(d) Overlapping of schemes

21. Identify the incorrectly matched pair.

	Rivers	**Tributaries**
(a)	Indus	– Sutlej
(b)	Ganga	– Yamuna
(c)	Brahmaputra	– Krishna
(d)	Godavari	– Manjra

22. What does social exclusion denies to certain individuals?
(a) Facilities
(b) Benefits
(c) Opportunities
(d) All of the above

23. Name the islands belonging to the Indian Territory lies in the Bay of Bengal.
(a) Andaman and Nicobar Islands
(b) Sri Lanka
(c) Lakshadweep
(d) Maldives

24. Which of the following rights was/were not established as 'natural and inalienable' rights by the Constitution of 1791?
(a) Right to Life
(b) Freedom of Speech and Opinion
(c) Equality before the law
(d) All of the above

25. Complete the given analogy.
Nokrek Bio-Reserve : Meghalaya : :
Manas Bio-Reserve : ?
(a) Nagaland
(b) Assam
(c) Manipur
(d) Mizoram

26. Name the river which rises from the slopes of the Western Ghats in the Nasik district of Maharashtra.
(a) Mahanadi (b) Narmada
(c) Godavari (d) Koyna

27. What was/were the name of tax which was directly paid to the state by the Third Estate?
(a) Tithes (b) Livres (c) Taille (d) All of these

28. Most parts of India receive rainfall during which of the following months?
(a) December to February
(b) March to May
(c) June to September
(d) October to November

29. Identify the atmospheric condition(s) which governs the climate and associated weather conditions in India.

(a) Pressure and surface winds

(b) Upper air circulation

(c) Western Cyclonic Disturbances and Tropical Cyclones

(d) All of the above

30. Which of the following is responsible for the variation in the colour of soil in different parts of India?

(a) Difference in rock formations

(b) Weathering

(c) Erosion and deposition

(d) Land use

31. The region between .... and .... rivers is known as the Nepal Himalayas.

(a) Sarda, Koshi

(b) Ghaghara, Narayani

(c) Kali, Teesta

(d) Gandak, Kosi

32. Choose the incorrect statement about the River Narmada.

(a) It flows through a rift valley.

(b) It flows through a gorge near Jabalpur.

(c) It plunges over steep rocks at the Dhuadhar falls.

(d) Its tributaries are Tungabhadra and Musi.

33. Which of the following types of vegetation grows in areas with mean annual average temperature of above 24°C?

(a) Tropical (b) Subtropical

(c) Temperate (d) Alpine

34. What was/were the reasons for the Socialist Revolutionary Party's struggle?

(a) They struggled for peasants' rights.

(b) They demanded that land from nobles be transferred to them.

(c) Both (a) and (b)

(d) None of the above

35. Why did the Tsar dismiss the first Duma within 75 days of its election?

(a) Duma was incapable of taking good decisions.

(b) The Tsar did not want anyone to question his authority.

(c) The term of first Duma was of 75 days only.

(d) None of the above

36. Which of the following bodies was set up to try and prosecute the Nazi War criminals at the end of World War II?

(a) International Military Tribunal

(b) British Military Tribunal

(c) Allied Military Tribunal

(d) Allied Judicial Court

37. What does the given picture signify?

(a) Classroom in Germany depicting a lesson on racial Anti-Semitism.

(b) Classroom in Germany suggesting the proper teaching process of German students.

(c) The student explaining the numerical numbers.

(d) None of the above

38. Identify the policy followed by the British in India towards forests during the First and the Second World Wars.

(a) In India, working plans were abandoned during First and Second World War and the forest department cut trees freely to meet British war needs.

(b) Cutting of trees was strictly prohibited for everyone, including the British.

(c) More and more trees were planted to give employment to Indians.

(d) None of the above

39. Which of the following are the pastoral communities of Africa?

(a) Bedouins, Berbers (b) Maasai, Somali

(c) Boran, Turkana (d) All of these

40. In 1885, Massailand was cut into half with an international boundary between ....

(a) Kenya and Tanganyika

(b) Kenya and Ethiopia

(c) Congo and Angola

(d) Angola and Botswana

MCQs 2 Marks Questions

41. Match the following.

List I (Forests types)	List II (Annual rainfall)
A. Tropical Evergreen Forests	1. More than 200 cm
B. Moist Deciduous Forests	2. 100 to 200 cm
C. Dry Deciduous Forest	3. 70 to 100 cm
D. Tropical Thorn Forests and Scrubs	4. Less than 70 cm

Codes

	A	B	C	D		A	B	C	D
(a)	1	2	3	4	(b)	4	3	2	1
(c)	2	1	4	3	(d)	3	4	1	2

42. Name the peak which is marked as 'A' on the physical map of India.

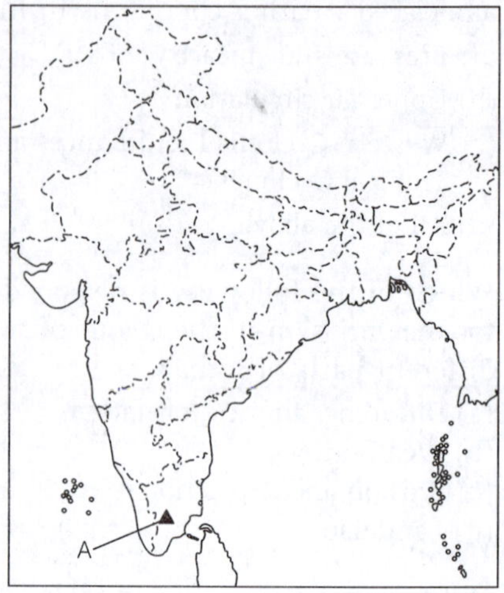

(a) Anai Mudi

(b) Mahendragiri

(c) Kanchenjunga

(d) Nanga Parbat

43. There are two statements marked as Assertion (A) and Reason (R). Mark your answer as per the codes given below.

Assertion (A) Food imports and previous years stocks may ensure food availability but the same cannot ensure food affordability.

Reason (R) Government can make the food available but for the affordability, an individual should have enough money to buy sufficient quantity and nutritious food.

Codes

(a) Both A and R are true and R is the correct explanation of A

(b) Both A and R are true, but R is not the correct explanation of A

(c) A is true, but R is false

(d) A is false, but R is true

44. Arrange the following in chronological order

I. Rebellion in the kingdom of Bastar
II. Kalanga uprising
III. Spread of Indian Railways
IV. Indian Forest Services set up

Codes

(a) I, II, III, IV
(b) II, IV, III, I
(c) II, III, IV, I
(d) III, IV, II, I

45. Read the passage and answer the following question.

The members of the Jacobin Club belonged mainly to the less prosperous sections of society. They included small shopkeepers, artisans such as shoemakers, pastry cooks, watch-makers, printers, as well as servants and daily-wage workers. Their leader was Maximilien Robespierre.

A large number of Jacobins came to be known as the 'sans-culottes'. What does it mean?

(a) People without knee breeches
(b) People with black shirts
(c) People with black trousers
(d) People without shirts

46. Consider the following statements associated with Poverty Line Estimation India.

I. In India, a minimum level of food requirement, clothing, footwear, fuel, lighting, educational and medical requirements, etc are determined for estimating the poverty line.
II. The food requirement while estimating the poverty line is based on the desired calorie requirement.
III. The calorie needs are different for every person depending on age, sex and the type of work.

Select the correct option.

(a) Only I
(b) I and II
(c) II and III
(d) All of the above

47. There are two statements marked as Assertion (A) and Reason (R). Mark your answer as per the codes given below.

Assertion (A) The Constituent Assembly was elected by the members of the existing provincial Legislatures.

Reason (R) The Constituent Assembly ensured a fair geographical share of members from all regions of the country.

Codes

(a) Both A and R are true and R is the correct explanation of A
(b) Both A and R are true, but R is not the correct explanation of A
(c) A is true, but R is false
(d) A is false, but R is true

48. Arrange the following in chronological order.

I. Proclamation of the Weimar Republic
II. Germany invaded the USSR
III. Treaty of Versailles

Codes

(a) III, II, I
(b) I, II, III
(c) II, I, III
(d) III, I, II

49. Read the given statements and select which ones are true (T) and which ones are false (F).

I. Election campaigning takes place for three week period between the announcement of final list of candidates and date of polling.

II. Election campaign means the promotion of the policies, offers and promises that the candidates make to the voters to fulfil, if they are elected.

III. In election campaigns, political parties try to focus public attention on some big issues.

Codes

	I	II	III		I	II	III
(a)	F	T	T	(b)	T	T	T
(c)	T	F	T	(d)	F	F	T

50. Identify the personality associated with the given extract.

"He wanted the government to encourage cooperatives and replace capitalist enterprises. These cooperatives were to be associations of people who produced goods together and divided the profits according to the work done by members."

(a) Louis Blanc (b) Karl Marx
(c) Robert Owen (d) Tsar

Darken your choice with HB Pencil

1.	ⓐ ⓑ ⓒ ⓓ	11.	ⓐ ⓑ ⓒ ⓓ	21.	ⓐ ⓑ ⓒ ⓓ	31.	ⓐ ⓑ ⓒ ⓓ	41.	ⓐ ⓑ ⓒ ⓓ
2.	ⓐ ⓑ ⓒ ⓓ	12.	ⓐ ⓑ ⓒ ⓓ	22.	ⓐ ⓑ ⓒ ⓓ	32.	ⓐ ⓑ ⓒ ⓓ	42.	ⓐ ⓑ ⓒ ⓓ
3.	ⓐ ⓑ ⓒ ⓓ	13.	ⓐ ⓑ ⓒ ⓓ	23.	ⓐ ⓑ ⓒ ⓓ	33.	ⓐ ⓑ ⓒ ⓓ	43.	ⓐ ⓑ ⓒ ⓓ
4.	ⓐ ⓑ ⓒ ⓓ	14.	ⓐ ⓑ ⓒ ⓓ	24.	ⓐ ⓑ ⓒ ⓓ	34.	ⓐ ⓑ ⓒ ⓓ	44.	ⓐ ⓑ ⓒ ⓓ
5.	ⓐ ⓑ ⓒ ⓓ	15.	ⓐ ⓑ ⓒ ⓓ	25.	ⓐ ⓑ ⓒ ⓓ	35.	ⓐ ⓑ ⓒ ⓓ	45.	ⓐ ⓑ ⓒ ⓓ
6.	ⓐ ⓑ ⓒ ⓓ	16.	ⓐ ⓑ ⓒ ⓓ	26.	ⓐ ⓑ ⓒ ⓓ	36.	ⓐ ⓑ ⓒ ⓓ	46.	ⓐ ⓑ ⓒ ⓓ
7.	ⓐ ⓑ ⓒ ⓓ	17.	ⓐ ⓑ ⓒ ⓓ	27.	ⓐ ⓑ ⓒ ⓓ	37.	ⓐ ⓑ ⓒ ⓓ	47.	ⓐ ⓑ ⓒ ⓓ
8.	ⓐ ⓑ ⓒ ⓓ	18.	ⓐ ⓑ ⓒ ⓓ	28.	ⓐ ⓑ ⓒ ⓓ	38.	ⓐ ⓑ ⓒ ⓓ	48.	ⓐ ⓑ ⓒ ⓓ
9.	ⓐ ⓑ ⓒ ⓓ	19.	ⓐ ⓑ ⓒ ⓓ	29.	ⓐ ⓑ ⓒ ⓓ	39.	ⓐ ⓑ ⓒ ⓓ	49.	ⓐ ⓑ ⓒ ⓓ
10.	ⓐ ⓑ ⓒ ⓓ	20.	ⓐ ⓑ ⓒ ⓓ	30.	ⓐ ⓑ ⓒ ⓓ	40.	ⓐ ⓑ ⓒ ⓓ	50.	ⓐ ⓑ ⓒ ⓓ

Practice Set 03

Time : 60 Mins. Max. Marks : 60

General Instructions

1. This question paper contains 50 questions.
2. All questions are compulsory. There is no negative marking.
3. Q. No. 1 to 40 are of 1 mark each and Q. No. 41 to 50 are of 2 marks each.
4. Use HB pencil / Blue ball point pen to mark your choice of answer by darkening the circles on the OMR Sheet.

MCQs 1 Mark Questions

1. Identify the form of government in which the rulers are elected by the people.

(a) Dictatorship
(b) Non-democratic Government
(c) Monarchy
(d) Democracy

2. Which party always won elections in Mexico since its Independence in 1930 until 2000?

(a) Revolutionary Party
(b) Mexican Revolutionary Party
(c) Institutional Revolutionary Party
(d) Institutional Party

3. Who among the following was the first captain of the National Hockey Team who was also the member of the Constituent Assembly ?

(a) Jaipal Singh
(b) Baldev Singh
(c) Somnath Lahiri
(d) KM Munshi

4. The Preamble to the Constitution of India declares India to be a ....

(a) sovereign, democratic, republic
(b) sovereign, socialist, secular, democratic, republic
(c) sovereign, socialist, democratic, republic
(d) None of the above

5. Which is not a part of the district and local level bodies?

(a) Panchayats (b) Municipalities
(c) Corporations (d) Lok Sabha

6. 'Save Democracy' slogan was given by which of the following political party in 1977 Lok Sabha elections?

(a) Congress Party (b) Janata Party
(c) Telugu Desam Party (d) Left Front

7. What is meant by 'Office Memorandum'?

(a) Order issued by the Government of India
(b) Memoirs of the leaders of the past
(c) Important defence documents
(d) None of the above

8. Who is the Supreme Commander of the defence forces of India?
(a) Parliament
(b) President
(c) Prime Minister
(d) Chief Minister

9. What was the result of the intervention of other countries to stop the killings of Albanians?
(a) Milosevic lost power and was tried for crimes against humanity.
(b) The other countries were punished by UNO for interfering in another country.
(c) Led to further army action by Milosevic.
(d) None of the above

10. Which of the following terms is correct for the feature of the Indian Constitution stating that no person is above the law?
(a) State of Law
(b) Application of Law
(c) Rule of Law
(d) Governance by Law

11. What do you mean by Bigha and Guintha?
(a) The measuring units of grain
(b) The types of hybrid seeds
(c) The measuring units of land area in the village
(d) The type of village house

12. The activities such as small manufacturing, transport, shopkeeping, etc are referred to as ....
(a) non-economic activities
(b) non-farming activities
(c) non-traditional activities
(d) non-market activities

13. Which of the following is a significant step towards providing elementary education to all the children in the age group of 6-14 years?
(a) Sarva Shiksha Abhiyan
(b) Adult Education Programme
(c) Mid-day Meal Scheme
(d) None of the above

14. Disguised unemployment occurs when the number of persons working on a farm is ....
(a) only what is required
(b) more than required
(c) less than required
(d) None of the above

15. In which part of the country, grain banks have been set up by NGO's?
(a) Gujarat (b) Haryana
(c) Punjab (d) Maharashtra

16. What do you understand by the Marginal farmers?
(a) Farmers who use modern methods for farming.
(b) Farmers who practice crop rotation for farming.
(c) Farmers who did not have sufficient land for farming.
(d) Farmers who use modern methods for irrigation.

17. The death of a child under the age of .... is called Infant Mortality Rate.
(a) 1 year (b) 2 years
(c) 3 years (d) 4 years

18. In which state, the land reform measures helped to reduce poverty?
(a) Tamil Nadu (b) Punjab
(c) West Bengal (d) Kerala

19. Why the calorie requirement is higher in the rural areas than urban areas?

(a) People of rural areas do not enjoy as much as people in the urban areas.
(b) People of rural areas are not health conscious.
(c) People are engaged in mental work in rural areas.
(d) Because the people are engaged in physical labour in rural areas.

20. Choose the title that closely relates to the given picture.

(a) Self- sufficiency in food grains
(b) Fair price shop
(c) Massive starvation and food insecurity
(d) Types of hunger

21. For what purpose, the representatives of the Third Estate assembled in the indoor tennis court of Versailles on 20th June ?

(a) Hunger strike
(b) Drafting a Constitution for France which limited the king's power.
(c) Declaring a revolt
(d) Making an appeal to support the king in times of need.

22. Identify the provisions which form a part of the 'Declaration of Rights of Man and Citizen'.

(a) Men are born free.
(b) They are equal in rights before the law.
(c) Liberty means powers to do what is not injurious to others.
(d) All of the above

23. Identify the incorrect statement about the 'radicals'.

(a) They supported women's Right to Vote.
(b) They opposed the privileges of great landowners.
(c) They were completely against the existence of private property.
(d) None of the above

24. Why most of the Bolshevik Party members initially surprised by 'April Theses'?

(a) They wanted continuation of World War I.
(b) They thought that time was not ripe for a socialist revolution.
(c) Government needed to be supported at this time.
(d) All of the above

25. According to the Nazis, which people were to be regarded as desirable?

(a) Pure and healthy Nordic Aryans.
(b) German soldiers who helped in territorial expansion.
(c) German police of different types.
(d) All those who were willing to consider Hitler as God.

26. When did the Colonial Government in India passed the Criminal Tribes Act?

(a) 1875
(b) 1860
(c) 1871
(d) 1840

27. Why Colonial rulers considered forests as unproductive?

(a) The forests were not fit for habitation.
(b) The forests had wild grown trees only.
(c) The forests did not yield revenue to enhance income of the state.
(d) The forests were full of wild animals.

28. What does the picture depict?

(a) Jewish students are expelled from school.
(b) Jewish teacher and students are expelled from school.
(c) Racism is introduced in Nazi school.
(d) Jewish teacher and Jewish people are expelled from school under the jeers of German classmates.

29. What was/were the result of overgrazing pastures due to restrictions on Pastoral Movements?
(a) The quality of pastures declined.
(b) Pastoral Movements created deterioration of animal stock.
(c) Underfed cattle died in large numbers during scarcity and famine.
(d) All of the above

30. Which of the following is the longitudinal extent of India?
(a) 8°4′ N and 37°6′ N
(b) 68°7′ N and 97°25′ E
(c) 68°7′ E and 97°25′ W
(d) 8°4′ E and 37°6′ E

31. Due to which of the following reasons is/are the Indian Ocean named after India?
(a) India has a strategic location along the trans-Indian Ocean routes.
(b) No other country has a long coastline on the Indian Ocean as India.
(c) India is centrally located at the head of the Indian Ocean.
(d) All of the above

32. A landmass bounded by sea on three sides is referred to as ....
(a) coast
(b) island
(c) peninsula
(d) None of the above

33. Identify the incorrectly matched pair.
(a) Luni River – In the Indian desert
(b) Kaveri River – Forms delta in the Northern circar
(c) Anai Mudi – Highest peak in the Western Ghat
(d) Baghelkhand – Eastward extension of the Central highlands

34. Arrange the following rivers in descending order as per their length.
(a) Indus , Ganga, Mahanadi, Kaveri
(b) Kaveri, Mahanadi, Indus, Ganga
(c) Indus, Kaveri, Mahanadi , Ganga
(d) Kaveri, Indus, Ganga, Mahanadi

35. Which kind of a drainage pattern is formed when tributaries join rivers at almost right angles?
(a) Dendritic drainage
(b) Trellis drainage
(c) Rectangular drainage
(d) Radial drainage

36. During which months, Tamil Nadu coast get most of its rainfall?
(a) December to February
(b) March to May
(c) June to September
(d) October to November

37. By October, the Dhangars harvested their bajra and started on their move to the West. Why were they welcomed by the Konkani peasants?

(a) The Dhangars married off their children in each others communities.
(b) The Dhangars brought bajra for them.
(c) Dhangar flocks manured their fields and fed on the stubble.
(d) None of the above

38. Complete the given analogy.
Tropical Evergreen Forests : Mahogany : : ? : Teak.

(a) Moist Deciduous Forests
(b) Montane Forests
(c) Mangrove Forests
(d) Tropical Thorn Forests and Scrubs

39. The rate or pace of population increase per year is referred to as which of the following?

(a) Absolute increase
(b) Magnitude of increase
(c) Annual Growth Rate
(d) Population change

40. Identify the reason(s) which is/are responsible for uneven population distribution in India.

(a) Variations in topography or relief in different parts of India.
(b) Variations in climate and rainfall distribution.
(c) Variations in the rate of industrialisation and urbanisation.
(d) All of the above

MCQs 2 Marks Questions

41. With the help of given map of India name the river which is marked as 'A'.

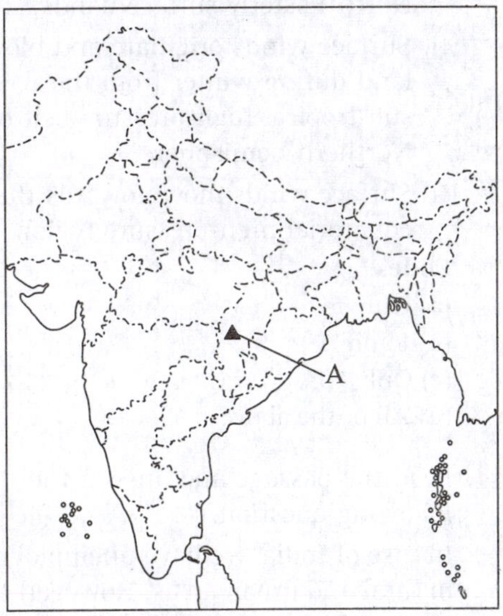

(a) Mahanadi River (b) Tapi River
(c) Bhima River (d) Godavari River

42. Match the following.

List I (Biosphere)	List II (Location)
A. Seshachalam	1. Andhra Pradesh
B. Panna	2. Madhya Pradesh
C. Kanchenjunga	3. Sikkim
D. Nanda Devi	4. Uttarakhand

Codes

	A	B	C	D		A	B	C	D
(a)	1	2	3	4	(b)	4	3	2	1
(c)	2	1	4	3	(d)	3	4	1	2

43. Find the correct option about pressure and surface wind.

I. India lies in the region of the North-Easterly surface winds.

II. Surface winds originate and blow over land during winter from the sub-tropical high-pressure belt of the Northern hemisphere.

III. Surface winds move towards the equatorial high-pressure region.

Codes

(a) Only I

(b) I and II

(c) Only III

(d) All of the above

44. Read the passage and answer the following question.

In case of India, we have unemployment in rural and urban areas. However, the nature of unemployment differs in rural and urban areas. In case of rural areas, there is seasonal and disguised unemployment. Urban areas have mostly educated unemployment. Seasonal unemployment happens when people are not able to find jobs during some months of the year.

People dependent upon agriculture usually face such kind of problem.

The persons who are not working by choice are covered under which of the following unemployments?

(a) Seasonal unemployment

(b) Disguised unemployment

(c) Educated unemployment

(d) None of the above

45. There are two statements marked as Assertion (A) and Reason (R). Mark your answer as per the codes given below.

Assertion (A) Economic growth widens (increase in scope/area) opportunities and provides the resources needed to invest in human development.

Reason (R) High economic growth encourages people to send their children (including the girl child) to school with hope of better economic returns from investing in education.

Codes

(a) Both A and R are true and R is the correct explanation of A

(b) Both A and R are true, but R is not the correct explanation of A

(c) A is true, but R is false

(d) A is false, but R is true

46. Arrange the following in a correct sequence.

I. A formal decision for implementation of Mandal Commission.

II. Appointment of Second Backward Classes Commission by Government of India.

III. Mandal Commission gave its report and recommendations.

Codes

(a) II, III, I

(b) I, II, III

(c) III, I, II

(d) I, III, II

47. Read the following statements about Right to Education and select which ones are true (T) and which ones are false (F).

I. Article 21-A of the Indian Constitution deals with the Right to Education.

II. The Article 21-A says that state shall provide free and compulsory education to all children of the age of 6 to 14 years.

III. It came into force on 1st April, 2010.

IV. It enforces Education as a Fundamental Right (Article 21).

Codes

	I	II	III	IV		I	II	III	IV
(a)	T	T	T	T	(b)	T	T	T	F
(c)	T	F	T	F	(d)	F	F	T	T

48. Read the passage and answer the following question.

It comprised of the group of persons, who have special functions in the Church. They owned vast land and wealth. They enjoyed certain privileges by birth, like exemption from paying taxes to the state. The Church levied a tax, called Tithe from the peasants which comprised of one-tenth of the agricultural produce.

Who among the following was/were associated with this?

(a) First Estate (the clergy)
(b) Second Estate (the nobility)
(c) Third Estate
(d) Both (a) and (c)

49. Identify the incorrectly matched pair.

I. Karl Marx	–	Father of communism
II. Lenin	–	Leader of Bolshevik Party
III. Stalin	–	Collectivisation Programme
IV. Nicholas ll	–	Tsar of France

Codes

(a) Only I
(b) Both II and III
(c) Only IV
(d) None of these

50. There are two statements marked as Assertion (A) and Reason (R). Mark your answer as per the codes given below.

Assertion (A) In Nazi Germany, young people and even children were repeatedly told that women were radically different from men.

Reason (R) Boys were taught to be aggressive, masculine and hardworking while girls were told to become good mothers and bring up pure-blooded Aryan children.

Codes

(a) Both A and R are true and R is the correct explanation of A
(b) Both A and R are true, but R is not the correct explanation of A
(c) A is true, but R is false
(d) A is false, but R is true

Darken your choice with HB Pencil

1.	ⓐ ⓑ ⓒ ⓓ	11.	ⓐ ⓑ ⓒ ⓓ	21.	ⓐ ⓑ ⓒ ⓓ	31.	ⓐ ⓑ ⓒ ⓓ	41.	ⓐ ⓑ ⓒ ⓓ
2.	ⓐ ⓑ ⓒ ⓓ	12.	ⓐ ⓑ ⓒ ⓓ	22.	ⓐ ⓑ ⓒ ⓓ	32.	ⓐ ⓑ ⓒ ⓓ	42.	ⓐ ⓑ ⓒ ⓓ
3.	ⓐ ⓑ ⓒ ⓓ	13.	ⓐ ⓑ ⓒ ⓓ	23.	ⓐ ⓑ ⓒ ⓓ	33.	ⓐ ⓑ ⓒ ⓓ	43.	ⓐ ⓑ ⓒ ⓓ
4.	ⓐ ⓑ ⓒ ⓓ	14.	ⓐ ⓑ ⓒ ⓓ	24.	ⓐ ⓑ ⓒ ⓓ	34.	ⓐ ⓑ ⓒ ⓓ	44.	ⓐ ⓑ ⓒ ⓓ
5.	ⓐ ⓑ ⓒ ⓓ	15.	ⓐ ⓑ ⓒ ⓓ	25.	ⓐ ⓑ ⓒ ⓓ	35.	ⓐ ⓑ ⓒ ⓓ	45.	ⓐ ⓑ ⓒ ⓓ
6.	ⓐ ⓑ ⓒ ⓓ	16.	ⓐ ⓑ ⓒ ⓓ	26.	ⓐ ⓑ ⓒ ⓓ	36.	ⓐ ⓑ ⓒ ⓓ	46.	ⓐ ⓑ ⓒ ⓓ
7.	ⓐ ⓑ ⓒ ⓓ	17.	ⓐ ⓑ ⓒ ⓓ	27.	ⓐ ⓑ ⓒ ⓓ	37.	ⓐ ⓑ ⓒ ⓓ	47.	ⓐ ⓑ ⓒ ⓓ
8.	ⓐ ⓑ ⓒ ⓓ	18.	ⓐ ⓑ ⓒ ⓓ	28.	ⓐ ⓑ ⓒ ⓓ	38.	ⓐ ⓑ ⓒ ⓓ	48.	ⓐ ⓑ ⓒ ⓓ
9.	ⓐ ⓑ ⓒ ⓓ	19.	ⓐ ⓑ ⓒ ⓓ	29.	ⓐ ⓑ ⓒ ⓓ	39.	ⓐ ⓑ ⓒ ⓓ	49.	ⓐ ⓑ ⓒ ⓓ
10.	ⓐ ⓑ ⓒ ⓓ	20.	ⓐ ⓑ ⓒ ⓓ	30.	ⓐ ⓑ ⓒ ⓓ	40.	ⓐ ⓑ ⓒ ⓓ	50.	ⓐ ⓑ ⓒ ⓓ

Answer Sheet

Chapter 01

1. (a)	2. (b)	3. (c)	4. (b)	5. (b)	6. (a)	7. (a)	8. (a)	9. (b)	10. (b)
11. (a)	12. (a)	13. (b)	14. (c)	15. (c)	16. (a)	17. (a)	18. (c)	19. (c)	20. (b)
21. (b)	22. (b)	23. (a)	24. (b)	25. (a)	26. (a)	27. (a)	28. (a)	29. (b)	30. (b)
31. (d)	32. (a)	33. (a)							

Chapter 02

1. (a)	2. (a)	3. (c)	4. (a)	5. (a)	6. (a)	7. (b)	8. (b)	9. (a)	10. (a)
11. (c)	12. (a)	13. (b)	14. (a)	15. (b)	16. (b)	17. (d)	18. (a)	19. (a)	20. (a)
21. (b)	22. (c)	23. (b)	24. (b)	25. (d)	26. (a)	27. (d)	28. (a)	29. (b)	

Chapter 03

1. (d)	2. (d)	3. (d)	4. (b)	5. (b)	6. (c)	7. (c)	8. (b)	9. (c)	10. (b)
11. (c)	12. (d)	13. (b)	14. (a)	15. (b)	16. (d)	17. (a)	18. (d)	19. (c)	20. (a)
21. (d)	22. (b)	23. (c)	24. (a)	25. (a)	26. (d)	27. (d)			

Chapter 04

1. (d)	2. (a)	3. (c)	4. (a)	5. (b)	6. (c)	7. (b)	8. (a)	9. (c)	10. (a)
11. (a)	12. (b)	13. (b)	14. (b)	15. (b)	16. (c)	17. (b)	18. (d)	19. (a)	20. (b)
21. (a)	22. (a)	23. (b)	24. (d)	25. (c)	26. (c)	27. (c)	28. (a)	29. (c)	30. (b)
31. (b)	32. (a)	33. (d)	34. (b)	35. (d)					

Chapter 05

1. (d)	2. (c)	3. (c)	4. (c)	5. (d)	6. (d)	7. (a)	8. (d)	9. (b)	10. (b)
11. (b)	12. (c)	13. (c)	14. (a)	15. (b)	16. (c)	17. (b)	18. (d)	19. (c)	20. (b)
21. (b)	22. (a)	23. (a)	24. (d)	25. (c)	26. (c)	27. (b)	28. (a)	29. (b)	30. (d)
31. (a)	32. (a)	33. (a)	34. (a)	35. (d)	36. (a)	37. (b)			

Chapter 06

1. (a)	2. (a)	3. (a)	4. (a)	5. (c)	6. (c)	7. (b)	8. (b)	9. (c)	10. (d)
11. (d)	12. (c)	13. (a)	14. (b)	15. (a)	16. (b)	17. (c)	18. (b)	19. (b)	20. (c)
21. (c)	22. (b)	23. (c)	24. (c)	25. (a)	26. (a)	27. (c)	28. (c)	29. (a)	30. (a)
31. (c)	32. (b)								

Chapter 07

1. (b)	2. (b)	3. (a)	4. (c)	5. (b)	6. (b)	7. (a)	8. (a)	9. (c)	10. (d)
11. (c)	12. (a)	13. (a)	14. (a)	15. (a)	16. (d)	17. (d)	18. (b)	19. (c)	20. (a)
21. (b)	22. (a)	23. (d)	24. (d)	25. (c)	26. (a)	27. (c)	28. (a)	29. (b)	30. (d)
31. (a)	32. (d)	33. (a)							

Chapter 08

1. (c)	2. (a)	3. (c)	4. (d)	5. (c)	6. (a)	7. (b)	8. (c)	9. (d)	10. (a)
11. (d)	12. (b)	13. (a)	14. (a)	15. (d)	16. (a)	17. (c)	18. (c)	19. (a)	20. (c)
21. (a)	22. (b)	23. (b)	24. (b)	25. (d)	26. (b)	27. (b)	28. (a)		

Chapter 09

1. (a)	2. (d)	3. (b)	4. (a)	5. (a)	6. (d)	7. (a)	8. (b)	9. (c)	10. (d)
11. (b)	12. (c)	13. (a)	14. (a)	15. (b)	16. (c)	17. (a)	18. (d)	19. (d)	20. (d)
21. (b)	22. (c)	23. (d)	24. (b)	25. (d)	26. (c)	27. (d)	28. (a)	29. (c)	

Chapter 10

1. (c)	2. (a)	3. (d)	4. (a)	5. (a)	6. (b)	7. (a)	8. (a)	9. (c)	10. (d)
11. (b)	12. (a)	13. (c)	14. (a)	15. (d)	16. (d)	17. (c)	18. (a)	19. (d)	20. (d)
21. (d)	22. (a)	23. (b)	24. (d)	25. (d)					

Chapter 11

1. (a)	2. (a)	3. (d)	4. (b)	5. (d)	6. (b)	7. (c)	8. (d)	9. (b)	10. (a)
11. (a)	12. (b)	13. (b)	14. (a)	15. (b)	16. (d)	17. (d)	18. (c)	19. (d)	20. (b)
21. (b)	22. (a)	23. (a)	24. (b)	25. (a)	26. (d)	27. (a)	28. (c)	29. (c)	30. (c)
31. (d)	32. (d)	33. (c)	34. (a)	35. (a)	36. (b)				

Chapter 12

1. (a)	2. (c)	3. (d)	4. (c)	5. (c)	6. (a)	7. (c)	8. (b)	9. (a)	10. (c)
11. (d)	12. (a)	13. (a)	14. (d)	15. (c)	16. (a)	17. (b)	18. (c)	19. (b)	20. (d)
21. (d)	22. (a)	23. (b)	24. (c)	25. (d)	26. (d)	27. (a)	28. (c)	29. (d)	30. (d)
31. (b)	32. (c)	33. (a)	34. (b)						

Chapter 13

1. (c)	2. (d)	3. (c)	4. (a)	5. (d)	6. (d)	7. (c)	8. (c)	9. (a)	10. (d)
11. (b)	12. (c)	13. (a)	14. (d)	15. (d)	16. (b)	17. (c)	18. (a)	19. (d)	20. (d)
21. (b)	22. (a)	23. (a)	24. (b)						

Chapter 14

1. (d)	2. (b)	3. (c)	4. (a)	5. (a)	6. (a)	7. (c)	8. (a)	9. (b)	10. (d)
11. (d)	12. (d)	13. (c)	14. (a)	15. (a)	16. (c)	17. (a)	18. (c)	19. (d)	20. (d)
21. (a)	22. (b)	23. (c)	24. (a)	25. (c)	26. (a)				

Chapter 15

1. (d)	2. (a)	3. (a)	4. (c)	5. (b)	6. (b)	7. (d)	8. (d)	9. (a)	10. (a)
11. (d)	12. (a)	13. (c)	14. (b)	15. (b)	16. (d)	17. (c)	18. (d)	19. (d)	20. (a)
21. (a)	22. (d)	23. (c)	24. (b)	25. (d)	26. (a)	27. (d)	28. (a)	29. (a)	30. (d)
31. (a)	32. (a)	33. (c)	34. (b)	35. (a)					

Practice Set 01

1. (c)	**2.** (d)	**3.** (c)	**4.** (a)	**5.** (c)	**6.** (b)	**7.** (a)	**8.** (b)	**9.** (c)	**10.** (a)
11. (a)	**12.** (b)	**13.** (a)	**14.** (a)	**15.** (a)	**16.** (c)	**17.** (a)	**18.** (c)	**19.** (d)	**20.** (a)
21. (a)	**22.** (d)	**23.** (d)	**24.** (c)	**25.** (a)	**26.** (a)	**27.** (b)	**28.** (b)	**29.** (a)	**30.** (d)
31. (b)	**32.** (c)	**33.** (d)	**34.** (a)	**35.** (b)	**36.** (a)	**37.** (a)	**38.** (c)	**39.** (a)	**40.** (b)
41. (a)	**42.** (a)	**43.** (d)	**44.** (a)	**45.** (a)	**46.** (c)	**47.** (d)	**48.** (b)	**49.** (a)	**50.** (a)

Practice Set 02

1. (c)	**2.** (a)	**3.** (c)	**4.** (b)	**5.** (d)	**6.** (c)	**7.** (b)	**8.** (a)	**9.** (a)	**10.** (c)
11. (d)	**12.** (c)	**13.** (b)	**14.** (a)	**15.** (b)	**16.** (a)	**17.** (b)	**18.** (d)	**19.** (a)	**20.** (c)
21. (c)	**22.** (d)	**23.** (a)	**24.** (d)	**25.** (b)	**26.** (c)	**27.** (c)	**28.** (c)	**29.** (d)	**30.** (a)
31. (c)	**32.** (d)	**33.** (a)	**34.** (c)	**35.** (b)	**36.** (a)	**37.** (a)	**38.** (a)	**39.** (d)	**40.** (a)
41. (a)	**42.** (a)	**43.** (a)	**44.** (c)	**45.** (a)	**46.** (d)	**47.** (a)	**48.** (b)	**49.** (a)	**50.** (a)

Practice Set 03

1. (d)	**2.** (c)	**3.** (a)	**4.** (b)	**5.** (d)	**6.** (b)	**7.** (a)	**8.** (b)	**9.** (a)	**10.** (c)
11. (c)	**12.** (b)	**13.** (a)	**14.** (b)	**15.** (d)	**16.** (c)	**17.** (a)	**18.** (c)	**19.** (d)	**20.** (c)
21. (b)	**22.** (d)	**23.** (c)	**24.** (d)	**25.** (a)	**26.** (c)	**27.** (c)	**28.** (d)	**29.** (d)	**30.** (b)
31. (d)	**32.** (c)	**33.** (b)	**34.** (a)	**35.** (b)	**36.** (d)	**37.** (c)	**38.** (a)	**39.** (c)	**40.** (d)
41. (a)	**42.** (a)	**43.** (c)	**44.** (d)	**45.** (b)	**46.** (a)	**47.** (a)	**48.** (a)	**49.** (c)	**50.** (b)